CHANGING
GEOGRAPHY

SERIES EDITOR: JANET SPEAKE

# Sustainable tourism

ALAN MARVELL
AND
CLAIRE WATKINS

## ACKNOWLEDGEMENTS

The authors would like to thank Dr Janet Speake and Dr Duncan Light (Liverpool Hope Univeristy College) for comments on an early draft of this book, Dr Simon Haslett (Bath Spa University College) for the Skyrail case study, Dr Janice Ross (Quality Assurance Agency for Higher Education) for the Maldives case study and Diane Wright (Geographical Association) for her encouragement and support in producing this book.

The Geographical Association is grateful to the individuals and organisations that have provided the images for this book.

AUTHORS: Alan Marvell is a Senior Lecturer in Geography and Course Director for Tourism Management at Bath Spa University College. Claire Watkins is a Postgraduate Researcher in Geography at the University of Gloucestershire.



**ISBN 1 84377 096 2**
**First published 2005**
**Impression number 10 9 8 7 6 5 4 3 2 1**
**Year 2008 2007 2006**

Published by the Geographical Association, 160 Solly Street, Sheffield S1 4BF. The Geographical Association is a registered charity: no 313129.

The Publications Officer of the GA would be happy to hear from other potential authors who have ideas for geography books. You may contact the Officer via the GA at the address above.

Edited by Tony Williams
Designed by Arkima Ltd, Leeds
Printed and bound in China through Colorcraft Ltd, Hong Kong

# CONTENTS

# EDITOR'S PREFACE

The books in the *Changing Geography* series seek to alert students in schools and colleges to current developments in university geography. The series also aims to close the gap between school and university geography. This is not a knee-jerk response – that school and college geography should be necessarily a watered-down version of higher education approaches – but as a deeper recognition that students in post-16 education should be exposed to the ideas currently being taught and researched in universities. Many such ideas are of interest to young people and relevant to their lives (and school examinations).

The series introduces post-16 students to concepts and ideas that tend to be excluded from conventional school texts. Written in language which is readily accessible, illustrated with contemporary case studies, including numerous suggestions for discussion, projects and fieldwork, and lavishly illustrated, the books in this series put post-16 geography in the realm of modern geographical thinking.

In order for tourism to develop, it has become increasingly apparent that it must be both economically successful and protective of the resources on which it depends. *Sustainable tourism* indicates that successful sustainable tourism approaches engender benefits for the people living in the destination, the tourist, the tourism company, governments and other organisations and, last (but by no means least) the environment. The challenge is to apply such approaches in mass tourism areas.

**Janet Speake**
**February 2005**

# INTRODUCTION

The rise in popularity of sustainable tourism has been brought about by a gradual change in the perception of both the tourism industry and consumers. An increased awareness of environmental or 'green' issues has meant that people are demanding products that are more environmentally friendly and ethically correct. This presents an interesting challenge to the tourism industry. It encourages tourist destinations and resorts, and the transport systems used to reach them, to become more sustainable.

*Sustainability* is the notion of using finite resources in a way that ensures they are preserved for the future. The key to a sustainable future is quality, and this includes maintaining the quality of the environment and the quality of life for people working in tourism and living in that place, while maximising the contribution of tourism to the economy. The priniciples of sustainable tourism state that we should 'take only pictures and leave only footprints', and 'think globally and act locally', in order to preserve the very resources that attract us to visit an area in the first place.

Chapter 1 explores the growth in global travel and the rise of alternative tourism. Most people who go on holiday are considered to be 'mass tourists' – they purchase a holiday 'package' that includes transport, accommodation and hospitality. Mass tourism destinations tend to cater for large numbers of visitors and can be found in typical 'summer sun' holiday brochures. Alternative forms of tourism such as eco-tourism operate with smaller numbers of visitors and are concerned to avoid the negative impact that large numbers of tourists can have upon the environment and local communities. Different definitions of sustainable tourism are introduced and compared in the light of changes in consumer expectation and the rise of local 'self-help' initiatives such as Agenda 21.

Chapters 2 and 3 suggest different ways in which the tourism industry, governments and local communities plan for a sustainable future. The relationship between transport, visitors, the environment and the local community is discussed, as without a positive relationship between these elements tourism will not be sustainable in the long term. Chapter 3 shows how resort planners use a range of techniques to carry out evaluations and suggest suitable strategies. Case studies from Northumberland National Park and Center Parcs show how sustainable tourism can be put into practice.

# INTRODUCTION

Chapter 4 explores the growth in eco-tourism and considers differences in the concept's interpretation and use. It also questions the extent to which eco-tourism can be considered sustainable, and provides examples from Belize and Costa Rica.

Chapter 5 considers the rise in the number of green awards and eco-labels that are used to show how consumer products – of which tourism is one – do less harm to the environment compared to others. The development of a European eco-label is discussed, as well as the use of existing green tourism awards. Case studies are drawn from the UK and Australia.

Chapter 6 brings together some of the key aspects of sustainable tourism and critically evaulates their use through contrasting case studies of Malta and the Maldives. Both countries have developed sustainable tourism strategies but their backgrounds and experiences have been very different.

# FROM MASS TO SUSTAINABLE TOURISM

## The expansion of global travel

Tourism has existed ever since people have had enough spare time and money to indulge in travel as a leisure pursuit. In the last 25 years there has been a dramatic increase in global tourist travel, with people travelling further and going on holiday more frequently. According to the World Tourism Organization (WTO), there were 694 million international tourist arrivals across the globe in 2003, compared with 687 million in 2000. In terms of its value worldwide, the tourism industry was estimated at US$514 billion (£277.4 billion) in 2003, the average spend per tourist being US$741 (£399.87) (WTO, 2004).

The majority of the world's tourists come from the industrialised countries of Europe, the Americas, East Asia and the Pacific, where people have relatively high levels of disposable income, leisure time, and the desire and freedom to travel. A similar geographical pattern can be seen in relation to tourist destinations, with France at the top of the list in terms of global share of tourist arrivals (Table 1). The term 'arrivals' does not include domestic tourists (tourists who travel within their own country on holiday); it refers only to international tourist arrivals, known as inbound tourists.

**Table 1: Top ten international tourist arrivals, by country, 2003. Source: WTO, 2004.**

| Ranking | Country | Arrivals (millions) |
|---|---|---|
| 1 | France | 75.0 |
| 2 | Spain | 52.5 |
| 3 | United States | 40.4 |
| 4 | Italy | 39.6 |
| 5 | China | 33.0 |
| 6 | United Kingdom | 24.8 |
| 7 | Austria | 19.1 |
| 8 | Mexico | 18.7 |
| 9 | Germany | 18.4 |
| 10 | Canada | 17.5 |

In its projections for the future growth of tourism (shown in Figure 1), the WTO estimates that by 2020 international tourist arrivals will exceed 1.56 billion. The top five tourist receiving areas are expected to be Europe, East Asia, the Pacific, the Americas and Africa.

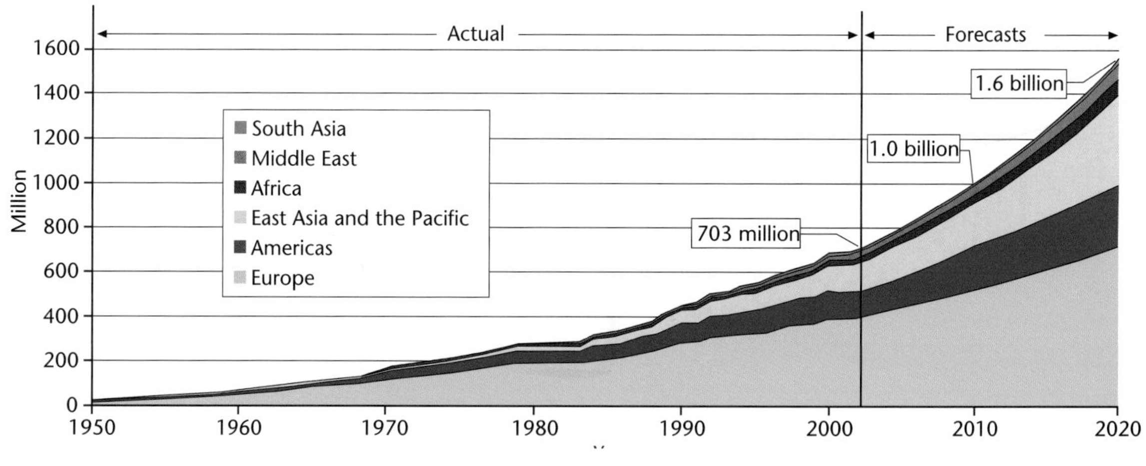


Figure 1: International tourist arrivals, 1950-2020. Source: WTO website.

**Activity Box 1: International tourist arrivals**

- Suggest reasons why France receives more inbound tourists than any other country in the world (see Table 1).
- Using the information shown in Figure 1, describe the growth in international tourism between 1950 and 2020.
- Give reasons to explain the rapid rise in the number of tourist arrivals over this period.
- For what reason did the tourist arrival figures drop sharply around 2001-02? Why do you think the numbers picked up again relatively quickly?

The dramatic increase in tourism in recent decades has led to 'mass tourism', which is itself a type of mass consumption, based on the principles of supply and demand and economies of scale. Mass tourism involves a large number of consumers (tourists) who purchase standardised products (package holidays). The more products (holidays) that are produced (supply), the cheaper they will become, and this in turn leads to a greater demand.

The consequences of mass tourism may be beneficial to some (e.g. tour operators, resorts, transport companies), but damaging in other ways. For example, it has already led to reductions in species diversity, to pollution of the environment, to the depletion of natural resources and to the decline in the aesthetic quality of certain highly popular tourist destinations. Over the last 25 years concerns relating to these negative impacts of tourism have led to a rise in 'alternative tourisms' and, associated with this, a wider implementation of the principles of sustainable tourism development.

### The rise of alternative tourisms

In the late 1970s and early 1980s the Alpine areas of Germany, Austria, Italy, Switzerland and France became increasingly popular destinations for tourists

Figure 2: Levant beach, Benidorm - mass tourism development on the coast of Spain. Photo: © www.travel-ink.co.uk.

**Information Box 1: Sustainability**

In 1987, the United Nations World Commission on Environment and Development produced a report entitled *Our Common Future*. It identified five basic principles of sustainability:

1. The idea of holistic planning and strategy making
2. The importance of preserving essential ecological processes
3. The need to protect both human heritage and biodiversity
4. The need to develop in such a way that productivity can be sustained over the long term for future generations
5. Achieving a better balance of fairness and opportunity between nations

In essence, the aims of sustainability are to 'conserve our natural resources in a world that is growing in population, with ever-increasing demands for food, water, shelter, sanitation, energy, health services and economic security' (Oliver and Jeffrey, 2002).

in search of rural leisure activities. But activities such as skiing and mountain walking made huge demands on the fragile mountain environments and caused widespread damage. Consequently, attention was focused on ways of managing tourism in order to limit its negative impact. Concepts such as 'green tourism', 'responsible tourism' and 'alternative tourism' began to surface, and soon became part of mainstream thinking.

An increase in media coverage of environmental issues (such as global warming and the depletion of the ozone layer), together with high-profile campaigns by Greenpeace and Friends of the Earth, has raised public consciousness of this area and helped to stimulate a more environmentally aware political response. In the UK all the main political parties have developed 'environment manifestos'. The fear was that unplanned rapid development of the type seen in southern Spain (e.g. in Benidorm and Torremolinos – see Figure 2) could cause lasting and irreversible damage in other parts of the world (e.g. the Caribbean and Africa) unless measures were taken to prevent it.

Other responses to mass tourism have come from Tourism Concern, which campaigns for ethically- and fairly-traded tourism, and the World Travel and Tourism Council (WTTC) which has developed the Green Globe Award to recognise best practice in sustainable tourism development. But what exactly is sustainability? While its origins can be traced back to the mid-nineteenth century, the concept of sustainable development is attributed to the Brundtland Report, named after the Scandanavian Prime Minister who chaired the United Nations World Commission on Environment and Development in 1987, as Information Box 1explains.

Sustainability has implications for the growth of tourism because it suggests a need to adopt practices that move away from mass tourism. As Owen *et al.* have pointed out, the 'notion of sustainable development recognises that the Earth's resources are finite [i.e. they will run out]' (1993, p. 463). Sustainable development is about preserving environments and about using sustainable principles to address development processes.

These ideas can be applied to tourism. For example, the organisation Visit Britain (a merger of the English Tourist Board and the English Tourism Council) is responsible for promoting Britain to overseas visitors and England to domestic tourists. It regards sustainability as an essential part of tourism management:

> **'Sustainable tourism is about managing tourism's impacts on the environment, communities and the economy to make sure that the effects are positive rather than negative for the benefit of future generations. It is a management approach that is relevant to all types of tourism, regardless of whether it takes place in cities, towns, countryside or the coast' (English Tourism Council, 2002).**

### Towards sustainable tourism

Applying the principles of sustainability to tourism acknowledges the need for long-term planning, policy and decision making, as well as the need to limit the use of finite resources. The UN's five principles of sustainability (Information Box 1) address both the human and natural environments. They also focus on the capacity of the physical environment to meet the demands made on it by economic activity, including tourism. They therefore combine ideas of ecological

### Information Box 2: Agenda 21 and tourism

Agenda 21 sets out an internationally agreed framework of action within which to achieve sustainable development on a global scale. The framework was adopted by 182 governments at the first Earth Summit in 1992. Agenda 21 focuses on the role of governments, businesses and educators in improving the quality of local environments. It directly affects tourism because it promotes sustainable development in environmentally sensitive areas in the following ways:

- Governments are encouraged to preserve areas of natural beauty and protect wildlife; to promote leisure and tourism activities that are environmentally friendly; and to use tourism as a way of helping to sustain local economies.
- Businesses are encouraged to adopt effective environmental policies and to ensure that they minimise their impact on the environment.
- Educators are encouraged to teach people of all ages about how making small changes to their daily lives can bring about long-term benefits to the environment.

Most of the activities related to Agenda 21 take place at a local or community level. Local governments have been encouraged to set up Agenda 21 networks. Local Agenda 21 initiatives are intended to improve local environments and foster a better quality of life for local communities. The intention is that, cumulatively, this will encourage better attitudes towards the environment and resources at a global level – hence the Agenda 21 slogan 'Think global, act local'.

and economic sustainability, which can be described as follows:

- Ecological sustainability relates to environmental and conservation strategies which aim to protect flora and fauna and reduce or restrict environmental damage caused by tourists and the growth of tourist resorts.
- Economic sustainability in the context of the tourism industry is about ensuring the economic viability and development of the industry, while satisfying the needs of tourists and related sectors.

One way of illustrating the impacts of planning for ecological and economic sustainability is to look at the local scale, especially in relation to Agenda 21 activities (see Information Box 2).

Critics of Agenda 21 suggest that the movement towards a sustainable future remains focused on trade and development. Money and resources are invested in solving local environmental problems through a cascade or 'trickle-down' mechanism. However, there is no guarantee that resources will be used effectively to address environmental issues at the local level, or even spent on environmental improvements at all.

The rise in global tourism in general, and mass tourism in particular, has resulted in organisations and countries seeking to develop 'greener' policies. Linked to this has been the global recognition of a need to address the economic and environmental impacts of human activities. This chapter has indicated the relatively recent rise in alternative approaches to dealing with the impacts of tourism through sustainable development. The next chapter looks at the ways governments, businesses and other organisations are beginning to plan for sustainable tourism.

### Activity Box 2: Agenda 21 and tourism

Identify and investigate Agenda 21 initiatives being carried out in your area. Consider the following questions:

- If a group or organisation is involved, what issues is it promoting?
- What activities are being carried out?
- In what ways might Agenda 21 initiatives encourage tourism in your local area?
- In your opinion how sustainable is this approach?

# CHAPTER 2

# APPROACHES TO PLANNING

Chapter 1 established that rapid growth in the tourism industry during the second half of the twentieth century led to a need for further growth to be managed in a sustainable way. This chapter examines ways that different groups have planned for sustainable tourism while maintaining places' appeal as tourist destinations and as homes for local communities.

**The tourism triangle**

All tourism, including sustainable tourism, is based on a triangular relationship between visitors, the local (host) community and the place/environment (Figure 3). Each of these elements impacts upon the others, so each one must be carefully managed. The transport visitors use to reach their holiday destinations must also be taken into account when planning for sustainable tourism. Transport choices have wider impacts in terms of economic investment and the use of environmental resources.

Ensuring that the natural environment is preserved is just a part of becoming more sustainable.

The earnings from tourism need to be carefully reinvested in an area in order to maintain its viability as a tourist destination. Sustainable practices also ensure that businesses are more likely to survive as they focus attention on the effective use and quality of resources.

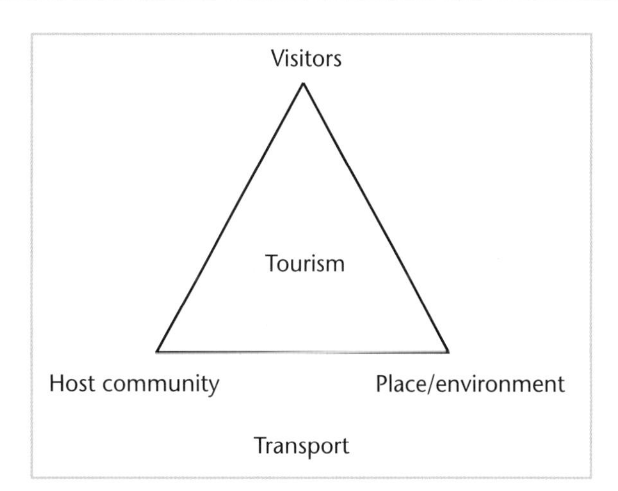


Figure 3: The Tourism Triangle.

**The influence of local communities**

The first stages of tourism development often go unnoticed, which gives rise to the perception that there is little need for planning. Sometimes early development is a reaction to demand. In a less economically developed country or in an area that is just beginning to realise its tourism potential, visitors will begin to expect a range of facilities that are not initially available (e.g. access to hospitality, accommodation and other services). Local people then begin to respond to the needs of visitors by developing services to meet those needs. This is demand-led tourism: it allows local communities to be involved and to benefit directly (e.g. Toledo Eco-Tourism Association, Case Study 3, page 27), but it remains sustainable only where the 'carrying capacity' of the area is not exceeded (see page20).

Alternatively, a government agency or a tour operator may identify tourism as a sustainable source of income for a community, leading to a planned or supply-led approach. Here an attempt is made to plan for the needs of tourists before they arrive. Prices may be set artificially high, to encourage small numbers of high-spending tourists to visit the area, which is often 'sold' on its exclusivity (the Costa Smeralda in the north-east of Sardinia is a good example of this kind of approach). However, developing an area for tourism before demand is established involves major investment and is considered a business risk. Smaller communities are unable to do it in isolation, and therefore often seek the assistance of governments and tour operators (e.g. the Maltese government, see Chapter 6).

The British Tourist Authority (2001) has stated that a community approach and community acceptance are essential if sustainable tourism is to succeed. This involves close partnership with local stake-holders, including community groups, business groups, landowners and local politicians, who may find it difficult to agree upon the bext way to plan for tourism development. Often differences of opinion between local groups need to be resolved before key

### Activity Box 3: Applying the tourism triangle

An 'all-inclusive' resort in the Dominican Republic. Photo: Diane Wright.

A rubber plantation in Thailand. Photo: Christina Leybourne

Ku-ring-gai Chase National Park, NSW, Australia. Photo: Diane Wright.

Prague, Czech Republic. Photo: Christina Leybourne.

Copy Figure 3 onto a large sheet of paper, and either imagine you have visited one of the places shown here or insert the name of a place you have visited. Think about each point of the tourism triangle in relation to that place and map out any concepts you think relate to that point. For example:

- **Visitor** – which activities did you take part in? How did each of these activities impact on ... the environment? ... the people living there...?
- **Local/host community** – how might your visit have benefited the environment or the local people? In what ways might it have had a negative impact? How did the activities of the local community affect the visitor?
- **Place/environment** – what features of the place/environment might most affect you as a visitor?
- **Transport** – what form(s) of transport were used to reach your destination? How might these impact on the local community and/or the environment (local as well as global)?

Label any inter-connections clearly and keep your concept map for future reference.

decisions can be made. This can cost both time and money, and if issues are not dealt with quickly resentment can build up. For example, during the 1990s, in order to increase the numbers of high-spending tourists to India, the government planned to expand the number of championship golf courses. Farmers, community groups and other non-governmental organisations feared that farming communities would lose their land and access to water supplies and receive little or no compensation.

To help prevent this sort of situation arising, Tourism Concern has produced 'Ten principles for community tourism' (see Information Box 3). The Toledo Eco-tourism Association (Case Study 3, page 27) provides an example of a community-led approach to planning tourism.

The tourism triangle is also influenced by the activities of the tourism industry itself and by the policies of national governments and international organisations.

**Information Box 3: Tourism Concern's 'Ten principles for community tourism'**

1. Community tourism should involve local people. That means they should participate in decision-making and ownership, not just be paid a fee.
2. The local community should receive a fair share of the profits from any tourism venture.
3. Tour operators should try to work with communities rather than individuals. Working with individuals can create divisions within a community. Where communities have representative organisations, these should be consulted and their decisions respected.
4. Tourism should be environmentally sustainable. Local people must benefit and be consulted if conservation projects are to work. Tourism should not put extra pressure on scarce resources.
5. Tourism should support traditional cultures by showing respect for indigenous knowledge. Tourism can encourage people to value their own cultural heritage.
6. Operators should work with local people to minimise the harmful impacts of tourism.
7. Where appropriate, tour operators should keep groups small to minimise their cultural and environmental impact.
8. Tour operators or guides should brief tourists on what to expect and on appropriate behaviour before they arrive in a community. That should include how to dress, taking photographs and respecting privacy.
9. Local people should be allowed to participate in tourism with dignity and self-respect. They should not be coerced into performing inappropriate ceremonies for the tourist.
10. People have the right to say no to tourism. Communities who reject tourism should be left alone.

Source: Mann, 2000, p. 25.

**Activity Box 4: Community tourism**

Using Tourism Concern's 'Ten principles for community tourism' (Information Box 3) and the Case Study of the Toledo Eco-tourism Association's approach to tourism development (page 27):

- Explain how a community approach benefits local people and the local environment in Belize.
- In your opinion, should a local community rely on tourism as its sole source of income? Give reasons for your answer.
- Explain which is more sustainable: a community-based approach, a government-led approach or an industry-led approach.
- Suggest reasons why an entirely community-led approach to tourism may be difficult to achieve.

## The tourism industry

The success of tourism is often measured by the number of visitors and the amount of revenue they generate, regardless of how efficiently resources are being used or how sustainable the tourism activity is. This can be seen in the nature and extent of official tourism statistics (e.g. on the Statistics on Tourism and Research UK (STAR UK) website). However, the need for sustainable forms of tourism has prompted the tourism industry to reconsider its strategies and to encourage the wiser use of resources. The industry has realised that unless it uses resources more efficiently, it has the potential to decline.

According to the British Tourist Authority (BTA), in order to be sustainable, tourism activity must comply with four key principles. These are:

1. *Visitor satisfaction* – visitors must be satisfied with all aspects of the tourism product
2. *Industry profitability* – the return to the industry must allow for reinvestment and growth
3. *Community acceptance* – account must be taken of the community's aspirations
4. *Environmental protection* – the resources on which the industry is based must be protected (BTA, 2001, p. 10).

BTA argues that only when all four of these principles are met can tourism become sustainable. But sustainable tourism policies must allow for variation between the expectations of the visitor and the local community, as well as taking account of the characteristics of the place itself (think back to the tourism triangle). What is regarded as being sustainable in one place may be inappropriate for another, so tourism policies must be tailored to each particular place. Also, developments in technology or attitudes among communities or visitors may change over time. Sustainable tourism, then, is a constant process of monitoring and action, and (according to BTA, 2001) sustainable tourism policies are best implemented locally at the level of the destination.

**The role of government**

The power to control the rate, location and type of tourist development (even community-based development) rests with national governments. However, local communities may resent what they see as a 'top-down' approach to planning, where decisions are made nationally or regionally. Often then a community-led approach is favoured because it is seen as meeting the needs of locals rather than imposing planning decisions that are in the nation's interest. In addition, entrepreneurs and businesses may see government policies restricting economic growth and seek to resist them. As a result, tourism development programmes now tend to be based on partnerships between government, business and the local community.

Inevitably, perhaps, economics also plays a part in national governments' attitudes towards tourism development. The government of a less economically developed country (LEDC) might create a tourism policy that focuses on economic objectives, including job creation, investment and development, to the detriment of the environment. Governments of more economically developed countries often prefer to promote environmental protection schemes in LEDCs, but such schemes may do little to address economic issues in the destination country. In effect, the priority given to environmental protection depends on the national government's philosophy and approach towards the environment.

Holden has identified four key areas where national and international policy can be used to help protect the environment:

1. 'The establishment of protected areas through legislation, for example national parks, and application for international recognition of significant environments, such as the World Heritage Site status awarded by UNESCO.
2. The implementation of land-use planning measures such as zoning, carrying capacity analysis, and limits of acceptable change to control development.
3. Mandatory use of environmental impact analysis for certain types of projects.
4. Encouraging co-ordination between government departments over the implementation of environmental policy, and entering into dialogue with the private sector to encourage the adoption of environmental management policies, such as environmental auditing and the development of environmental management systems' (Holden, 2000, p. 130).

The next section provides examples of the ways in which these principles are put into practice.

**Increased co-ordination**

Government departments are uniquely able to co-ordinate the various groups involved with tourism and to produce a policy for tourism development that is sustainable. As tourism comprises many different industries, co-ordination is sometimes difficult, and some governments have been preoccupied with encouraging visitors for economic reasons. The UK Government has produced *Tomorrow's Tourism* (Department for Culture, Media and Sport, 1999), which recognises the importance of sustainable development through tourism. Its own departments are required to work together to realise the Government's aims. For example, the UK Department for Culture, Media and Sport 'looks to promote the sustainable development of tourism through working closely with the Department for Transport on transport, the Office of the Deputy Prime Minister on planning and the Department for Environment, Food and Rural Affairs with respect to wildlife and countryside and rural development policies' (DCMS website). Public- and private-sector bodies are encouraged to help implement government policies.

The UK Government has introduced initiatives designed to protect sensitive areas, including National Parks and Country Parks, during the mid-twentieth century. Other smaller-scale designations, such as areas of outstanding natural beauty (AONBs) and sites of special scientific interest (SSSIs), were introduced in the late twentieth century. (AONBs and SSSIs usually relate to particular features within a locality or area and may lie within National or Country Parks.)

*National Parks*

Yellowstone, in the USA, was the first area to be designated a National Park in 1872 – 'for the purposes of leisure and recreation'. In England and Wales there are eleven National Parks; ten were established as a result of the National Parks and Access to Countryside Act in 1949. National Parks (see Case Study 1) are created to preserve wildlife, conserve areas of the countryside, and provide for recreation:

> **'National Parks protect examples of outstanding natural areas for educational, scientific and recreational use. They are the oldest form of environmental protection for natural areas and account for 57% of the world's protected areas' (Green and Paine, quoted in Newsome *et al.*, 2002, p. 190).**

National Scenic Areas were created in Scotland and perform a similar function to English and Welsh National Parks (see *Countryside Conflicts* – this series, Yarwood, 2002). The latest National Park to be officially recognised in England is the New Forest.

### Case Study 1: The Northumberland National Park sustainable tourism project

Northumberland National Park covers 1049 square kilometres and lies between the town of Hexham to the south and the border between England and Scotland to the north (Figure 4). It is the most remote and northerly of the National Parks in England and Wales. It is best known for the Roman-built Hadrian's Wall; because nearly a quarter of the Wall lies within the Park (Figure 5).

The area's remoteness affects the number of visitors, and recreation and tourism are not as highly developed as in the other National Parks in England and Wales. Although in a sense this is a benefit – there is little need for the construction of specialist visitor facilities, and less environmental damage such as footpath erosion caused by high volumes of walkers, there is also a cost – its inaccessibility reduces opportunities for farmers and local businesses and communities to gain extra income from tourism. The Northumberland National Park Authority has responded by developing a sustainable tourism strategy, which includes the following statement:

'The Sustainable Tourism Project aims to work with local people on the development and management of appropriate forms of tourist activities in the National Park. Initiatives include:

- Developing and promoting walking, cycling, painting or photography holidays using local people, skills and resources wherever possible
- Monitoring tourism activities in terms of their environmental impacts
- Raising money for conservation projects
- Communicating the purpose of the National Park to a wider audience through education and promotional literature.'

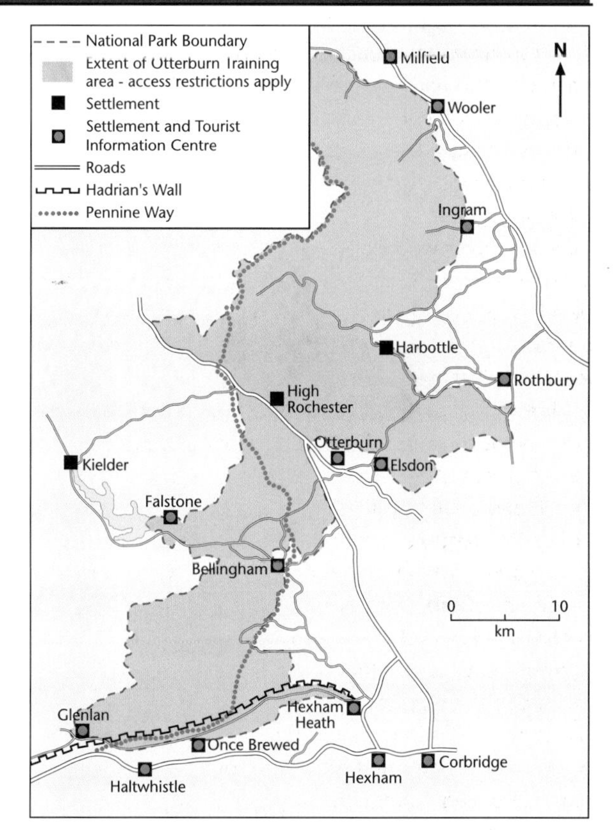


Figure 4: Northumberland National Park – location and access. Source: NNP website.

Sources: Northumberland National Park Authority, 2004; Council for National Parks, 1994.

Once a statement of intent on sustainable tourism

Figure 5: Images of Northumberland: Hadrian's Wall, cycle routes, Kielder Castle and the Cheviots. Photos: © Graeme Peacock.

is prepared, the relevant body – i.e. the National Park Authority – needs to implement it. In National Parks in France, for example, a land-use zoning approach to managing tourism is used (see Information Box 4).

Zoning can also be applied in marine environments by confining different recreational activities to specific areas. Activities such as swimming, wind surfing and jet-skiing are designated separate zones, thus taking account of noise and environmental issues as well as safety (see Chapter 6, pages 45-49)

**Protected areas and international organisations**

A number of international designations recognise unique environments: since 1972 the United Nations Educational, Scientific and Cultural Organization (UNESCO) has recognised World Heritage Sites as having significant cultural and/or natural importance. In promoting World Heritage Site status the organisation 'seeks to encourage the identification, protection and preservation of cultural and natural heritage around the world considered to be of outstanding value to humanity' (UNESCO, 2004). Currently 176 countries have signed the *Convention Concerning the Protection of the World Cultural and Natural Heritage*, and pledged to conserve these unique sites. Through the signing of an international agreement, the preservation of heritage for future generations becomes a responsibility shared by the international community as a whole.

This chapter has demonstrated how traditionally tourism development has either happened 'bottom-up' or 'top-down' (i.e. has either been community-based or driven by local or national government initiatives). While legislation continues to influence the type and extent of some tourism development (as well as protecting the natural beauty of an area), increasingly such development happens as a partnership between local communities and local

## Information Box 4: Land-use zoning

Land-use zoning is one of the oldest methods of town and country planning. Authorities designate each area as suitable for a particular use or mix of uses. This allows certain activities to be concentrated in one area: tourist facilities may be deliberately built at a distance from conservation areas. However, zoning can lead to the formation of tourist 'honey pots' (relatively small geographical areas that attract many visitors within a short period of time, like bees swarming round a pot of honey).

Some Mediterranean countries have adopted this policy along their coastlines, for example, Torremolinos and Benidorm in southern Spain have received investment for tourism development, while inland rural areas have not. An alternative approach is to disperse tourists across a larger area, thus minimising the negative effects of tourism and spreading the economic benefits to less-developed areas. In the short term this can result in more sustainable tourism; however, over time, several small pockets of intensive tourism often develop over a wider area.

National Parks in France usually contain two distinct land-use zones: a core or central zone and a buffer or peripheral zone (Figure 6).

1. In the core zone, protection of wildlife is the main objective. Activities in this zone are tightly controlled by the Park Authority, acting on behalf of the national government.
2. Recreation and tourism activities are permitted in the buffer zone, along with traditional rural industry and settlements. This zone is controlled using a higher degree of local community decision-making.

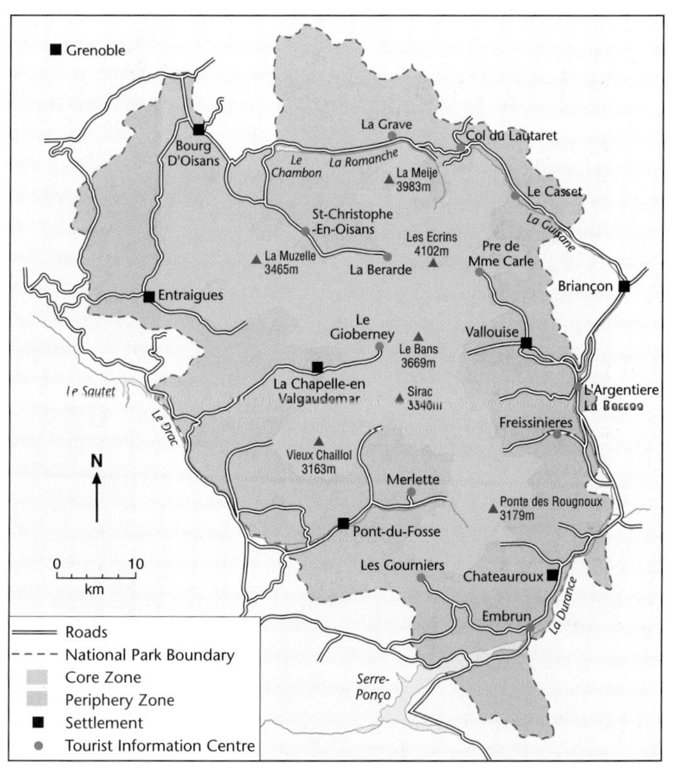

Figure 6: Land-use zoning in the Ecrins National Park, and images of the environment and visitor facilities in the core zone.

### Activity Box 5: Managing land use zoning in National Parks

Using Figures 4 and 5 and Case Study 1, decide whether it would be feasible to set up core and buffer or periphery zones in Northumberland National Park.

- Where might the activites described in this case study take place within the park boundaries?
- What special aspects of the Park would affect your decision?

Next, as a National Parks manager you have been instructed that the UK is to adopt the French system of core and periphery zoning as outlined in Information Box 4.

- Gather information on one National Park/National Scenic Area in the UK or another country and describe its sustainable tourism strategy.
- Using a map of your chosen National Park locate and identify its most visited areas and attractions.
- Which areas would be included in each zone? Justify your decisions.
- Do any of the most visited areas lie within your core zone? Describe how you would deal with visitor access to these areas.
- Present your findings using *PowerPoint*, and illustrate each of your zones with at least one image (see Figure 5).

### Activity Box 6: World Heritage Sites

Worldwide there are more than 750 cultural, natural or mixed sites on the World Heritage List. The UNESCO website has details of them all. You are to produce a report on a selection of World Heritage Sites.

- Choose either an area/region of the world or a particular type of property (e.g. cultural, natural or mixed) and look at a minimum of ten World Heritage Sites.
- For each one include: a description of the site and details of why UNESCO believes it should be preserved.
- Supplement the information on the UNESCO website with further information on each World Heritage Site from a variety of sources, and re-write the descriptions in your own words. You could illustrate your report on the area/region with images, maps and tables.
- In your report, describe the ways in which World Heritage designation could contribute towards sustainable tourism in each of the locations.
- Remember to include a list of sources.

The Tower of Belem. Lisbon, Portugal, is designated a World Heritage Site as are Stonehenge in the UK (inside front cover) and the temples of Ta'Hagrat and Mnajdra in Malta (page 42). Photo: Christina Leybourne

and national governments, and is influenced by international designations (e.g. in the formal recognition of unique environments by UNESCO). Therefore, it is increasingly the case that the planning of tourism developments must take account of all aspects of the tourism triangle – i.e. a development's impact on the environment, the local community, the experience of the visitor, and its effect at a global scale. The next chapter investigates the ways in which countries and tourism companies carry out audits and adopt environmental management systems to attain and retain sustainability in all of their activities.

# CHAPTER 3

# MODELLING SUSTAINABLE RESORTS

Chapter 2 demonstrated the range of strategies used by the tourism industry, local communities, governments and other organisations to plan for sustainable tourism. However, understanding the development of existing resorts can also help in planning future resorts on sustainable principles. This chapter shows how resort planners employ a range of tools to carry out evaluations and implement sustainable strategies.

### The Butler model

Butler has observed that tourist resorts often progress through five stages of development (Figure 7): the exploration state, the involvement stage, the development stage, the consolidation stage and the stagnation stage.

**Stage 1: Exploration.** Small numbers of to... because of area's natural and/or cultural features. No facilities are provided for visitors.

**Stage 2: Involvement.** Visitor numbers increase and become more regular. Some provision of tourist facilities. Limited advertising to attract tourists. Tourist season emerges.

**Stage 3: Development.** Development of a well-defined tourist market, partly shaped by a high degree of advertising. Local control of tourist facilities declines and is replaced by larger non-local organisations. Development of purpose-built tourist attractions.

**Stage 4: Consolidation.** Rate of increase in number of visitors declines. Major part of local economy is given over to tourism. Marketing is far reaching, especially in its efforts to extend the tourist season.

**Stage 5: Stagnation.** Capacity levels are reached, producing environmental, social and economic problems. Area no longer fashionable for certain holidays. Heavy reliance on repeat visitors. Much surplus capacity, requiring considerable effort to market the destination and attract new visitors.

Figure 7: The Butler model of resort and development. Source: Butler, 1980.

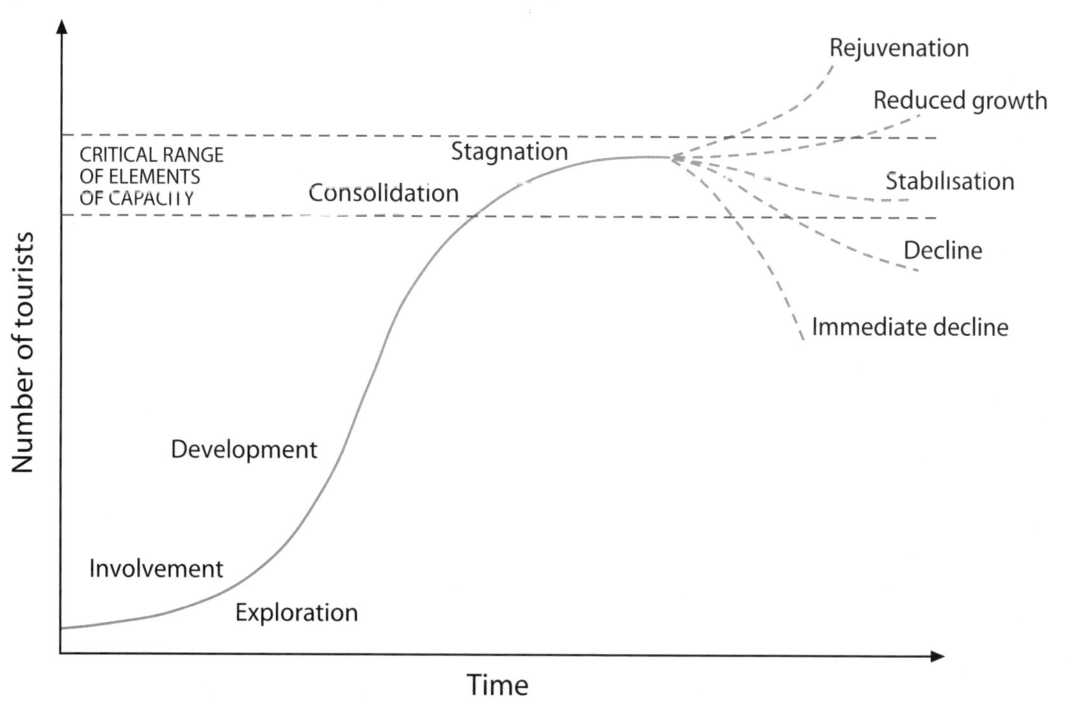

esorts progress through Butler's stages more
y than others, and, with careful planning, they can
ome sustainable. Butler recognises that a number of
esorts move beyond the fifth (stagnation) stage, so
'post-stagnation phases' have been added to the Model, as follows:

**Stage 6: Post-stagnation phases**

a. ***Rejuvenation*** – renewed growth and expansion of the resort
b. ***Minor adjustment*** – further growth of the resort, but at a much reduced rate
c. ***Readjustment*** – a reduced level of tourism development
d. ***No replacement of tourism facilities*** – a decrease in competitiveness results in a marked decline and no future in tourism.

(Adapted from Cooper *et al*., 2005; Williams, 1998.)

### *The Butler model and Barbados*

The evolution of tourism in a mature tourist destination, in this case Barbados in the Caribbean, can help illustrate the usefulness of the Butler model. Table 2 shows stop-over tourist arrivals to Barbados from independence in 1966 to 2002. In 1966, stop-over arrivals amounted to 79,104, and after this, the data reveals a boom-bust pattern, which accords with the Butler (1980) model. By 1997, the statistics for Barbados suggest it had 'broadly passed through the first five stages of the Butler model' (Dann and Potter, cited in Potter and Phillips, 2004, p. 241).

### *Carrying capacity*

The changing nature of tourism means that methods such as the Butler model have diminished in usefulness, and then been revised or further developed. Planners and tourism organisations now look at such issues as the carrying capacity of an area and the limits of acceptable change in terms of communities and environments; they also use environmental impact assessments and carry out environmental audits before and during tourism development.

When small numbers of people visit a newly emerging tourist destination their presence is often accommodated within the existing environment and infrastructure. As the resort becomes increasingly popular, damage to the environment can occur, and where the infrastructure (transport and communications systems, water supply, etc.) is stretched then the 'physical carrying capacity' has been exceeded. Geographers have also identified other types of carrying capacity, including:

- **Environmental or ecological carrying capacity** – the limits to which the environment can be used without severe erosion, noise pollution or litter becoming evident.
- **Economic carrying capacity** – the limits to which a local economy can safely be dependent on tourism.
- **Socio-cultural carrying capacity** – the limits to which an area can be used without causing negative impacts upon society or culture.

**Table 2: Stop-over tourist arrivals to Barbados, 1966-2000.**

| Year | Number of stop-over arrivals | Year | Number of stop-over arrivals | Year | Number of stop-over arrivals |
|---|---|---|---|---|---|
| 1966 | 79,104 | 1979 | 370,916 | 1991 | 394,222 |
| 1967 | 91,565 | 1980 | 369,915 | 1992 | 385,472 |
| 1968 | 115,697 | 1981 | 352,555 | 1993 | 389,428 |
| 1969 | 134,303 | 1982 | 303,778 | 1994 | 418,224 |
| 1970 | 156,417 | 1983 | 328,325 | 1995 | 434,247 |
| 1971 | 184,075 | 1984 | 367,652 | 1996 | 439,667 |
| 1972 | 210,349 | 1985 | 359,135 | 1997 | 461,470 |
| 1973 | 222,080 | 1986 | 369,770 | 1998 | 512,297 |
| 1974 | 230,718 | 1987 | 421,859 | 1999 | 517,870 |
| 1975 | 221,486 | 1988 | 451,443 | 2000 | 537,676 |
| 1976 | 224,314 | 1989 | 461,259 | 2001 | 497,852 |
| 1977 | 269,314 | 1990 | 432,092 | 2002 | 497,899 |
| 1978 | 316,883 | | | | |

**Activity Box 7: Cyclical tourism trends in Barbados**

- Using the statistics shown in Table 2, produce a graph of stop-over tourist arrivals in Barbados between 1966 and 2002.
- On your graph, mark periods of rapid growth, moderate growth and decline (there will be two of each), and the first five stages of the Butler model, and identify which post-stagnation phase of tourism is taking place in Barbados.
- Think about the influences that lead to changes to tourism in Barbados (e.g. tour operators, community-led tourism, destination-led tourism, government initiatives (see Chapter 2)), and wherever possible add notes on these to your graph.
- Using your graph, describe the cyclical nature of tourism in Barbados. (Bear in mind that changes in tourism can sometimes be attributed to global economic issues; for example, in both the early 1970s and the early 1980s there were crises in oil supply across the globe.)
- In your opinion, what implications would cycles of boom and bust have for the sustainability of tourism in Barbados after 2002?

- **Perceptual or psychological carrying capacity** – the limits at which local communities or visitors perceive that an area is overcrowded.

Carrying capacities are useful in calculating a maximum sustainable number of potential visitors to a specific area. Therefore, it is easier to apply these techniques to a National Park or a small island where the geographical boundaries are distinct and visitor numbers can be easily observed (see Case Study 1, page 15 and Chapter 6).

***Limits of acceptable change***

Rather than deciding upon the carrying capacity for a given area, tourism planners now use 'limits of acceptable change' for assessing tourism growth and development. In order to measure the 'limits of acceptable change', environmental indicators (e.g. water, soil and atmospheric quality) and social indicators (e.g. employment and perception towards tourists) are monitored over a given time period to obtain a record of the rate of change, and plan for future development.

This approach suggests that planners believe tourism development is inevitable; it does not allow them to question whether tourism is the best way to utilise resources, but seeks to regulate the rate of tourism development (as is the case with, for example, National Parks, see page 16).

***Environmental impact assessments***

Environmental impact assessments (EIA) have become a key part of the planning process in many countries. EIAs are associated with major projects such as the construction of roads, hotels and airports. Their aim is to minimise the effect of a development on the local environment and community by predicting the effect that it will have. EIAs assess the quality of the existing environment and the impact (both positive and negative) that, for example, a tourism development will have on it. Problems associated with the EIA approach are as follows:

- The environment is assessed on a project-by-project basis (with smaller projects not qualifying for such an assessment); thus, the incremental effects of development are not taken into account.
- The team carrying out the EIA may not use methods that involve local participation.
- The time taken to complete an EIA can cause delays in the planning process.

***Environmental auditing***

Environmental legislation enables companies to carry out an audit of their operations against specific indicators (e.g. pollution controls and sustainability initiatives). They can then implement environmental management systems (EMS). An environmental audit must cover all aspects of a business: directly from its own environmental impacts and indirectly via the policies of its suppliers. An audit forms part of the EMS. Companies benefit from regular reviews because audits often indicate ways in which resources can be used more effectively and thus result in cost savings (and they may be rewarded for their efforts – see Case Study 2 on page 23).

EMS are based on a philosophy known as the Deming Cycle (Figure 8), which is considered sound management practice (Collins, 2000). The Deming Cycle enables a company to set its targets for environmental management, put them into practice, check and monitor the process, and evaluate and act on any findings. This then leads into a repeat of the cycle.

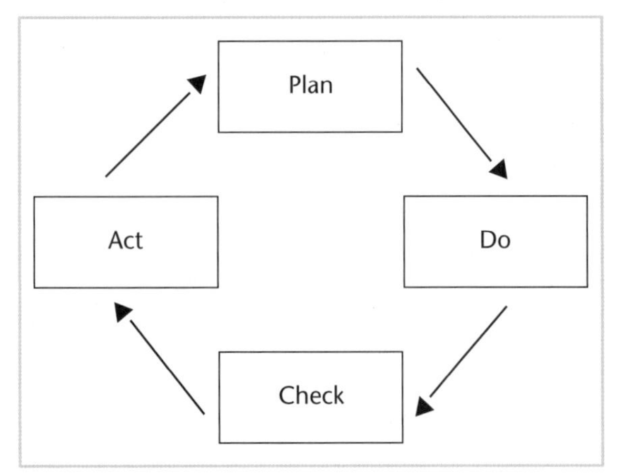


Figure 8: The Deming Cycle.

The International Standard (ISO 14001) provides opportunities for businesses to be internationally recognised for their EMS. In 1999 the leisure group Center Parcs (which offers holidays in specially constructed 'Villages') became the first such organisation in Europe to receive an ISO 14001. An important aspect of ISO 14001 is the successful management of an increase in biodiversity, which Center Parcs has achieved (see Case Study 2). Gratton (1997) suggests that Center Parcs has developed a three-stage approach to assessing the environmental impact of a Village:

- **Stage 1:** Detailed analysis of a site including an environmental impact assessment is carried out before applying for planning permission. If any environmental problems cannot be resolved then the site is not developed and alternative sites are located.
- **Stage 2:** Once construction is under way, the second stage is careful environmental monitoring of contractors to ensure that environmental protection and construction targets continue to be met.
- **Stage 3:** The final stage is when the Village is open to guests. This involves continual environmental monitoring to verify the sustainability of the Village environments when in daily use by guests. Training of staff is also important for ongoing care and maintenance in every aspect of their work to provide long-term sustainability (Gratton, 1997, pp. 11-13). (See Activity Box 8.)

### Activity Box 8: Planning a leisure village

Using information provided above and from the Center Parcs website you are asked to begin the search for a new leisure village location.

- You have been appointed by Center Parcs to develop a new holiday 'Village' in the UK. You must present your findings as an annotated map – which will form part of a display.
- You must identify an appropriate woodland or rural area within one hour's drive of a city or town of your choosing.
- Using your own knowledge and the information provided above, describe how you would carry out an environmental impact assessment. Think about the development's short-, medium- and long-term impacts on wildlife. How might you ensure that the existing wildlife does not abandon the site as soon as development commences (i.e. at Gratton's stage 2)? How might you attract wildlife to the Village in order to enhance the guests' experience (i.e. at Gratton's stage 3)? (Refer to the Deming Cycle in your answer.)
- How might you ensure that the Village attracts large numbers of visitors, while also ensuring that their activities have little impact on the environment? Look back at the information on Butler's Model, carrying capacity and the limits of acceptable change.
- Think about the location of the Village in terms of its proximity to existing settlements. What impact might it have on the local community?

Display all of the resulting maps and hold a class vote on which development would be most likely to win approval.

### Case Study 2: Center Parcs and the environment

Center Parcs originated in Holland and operates four sites in the UK: Elveden Forest, Longleat Forest, Oasis Whinfell Forest and Sherwood Forest. The company offers short-break holidays in rural woodland sites. Each site – known as a 'Village' – occupies approximately 162 hectares and includes accommodation, restaurants, bars, retail outlets, indoor and outdoor sporting facilities, an indoor (subtropical) swimming pool and a health and relaxation centre.

The natural environment is central to the Center Parcs concept and to the guests' experience of the Villages; it is therefore in the company's best interest to conserve and enhance any area it moves into. Environmental management procedures are aimed at continually improving and enhancing the Village environment and include an annual ecological monitoring process.

'Village' management covers both existing areas of ecological interest and areas which have potential to be enhanced. A full-time ecology manager and a landscape group ensure that management for wildlife at the Villages is co-ordinated in-house. With the help of Village environment teams, local naturalists and Wildlife Trust members, the company is able to monitor ecological matters and run its databases on wildlife in the Villages on a daily basis. Environmental consultants provide advice and training and undertake independent audits of Center Parcs's performance.

There have been increases in the populations of some of Britain's rarest plant and animal species across Elveden Forest, Longleat Forest and Sherwood Forest Villages. These Villages are home to 133 rare species of plants (including white horehound and knotted bur parsley) and birds (including osprey) and insects (e.g. woodland grasshopper). Deer sanctuaries are also a feature of the Villages, as are networks of lakes and waterways.

Source: Center Parcs, 2003.

Figure 9: The Center Parcs environment. Photos: © Center Parcs.

This chapter has demonstrated how tourism operators are able to utilise a variety of strategies to make decisions about and manage their activities in a more sustainable way. The next chapter shows how some of these ideas have been put into practice through eco-tourism. Eco-tourism emphasises the management of the environment as one of the main resources that draw tourists to a particular destination.

# CHAPTER 4

# ECO-TOURISM

Previous chapters have discussed the expansion of global travel, the impacts of tourism and the perceived necessity for sustainable approaches to planning and managing resorts. This chapter considers the costs and benefits of different types of eco-tourism to local communities, travellers, governments and tourism operators.

Eco-tourism has multiple definitions. It is referred to variously as 'alternative', 'responsible', 'green' and 'appropriate' tourism, all of which can, like 'sustainability' and 'sustainable tourism', be problematic in that such terms can be open to misinterpretation or manipulation. According to the Ecotourism Society, eco-tourism is:

> **'responsible travel to natural areas that conserves the environment and improves the well-being of local people' (1991, p. 1).**

And Honey defines eco-tourists as people who:

> **'travel to natural areas with a view to respecting, enjoying, and being educated about the natural environment and the culture of the local community in a manner that is low impact and sensitive to the long-term sustainability of these features' (1999, pp. 22-4).**

Both of these definitions indicate that eco-tourism is seen as a reaction or an alternative to mass tourism. Activity Box 9 offers a way of understanding issues related to eco-tourism and eco-tourists.

In order to understand eco-tourism more fully, we now can look at Honey's (1999) seven basic principles of eco-tourism. It

1. involves travel to natural destinations
2. minimises impact
3. builds environmental awareness
4. provides direct financial benefits for conservation
5. provides financial benefits and empowerment for local people
6. respects local culture
7. supports human rights and democratic movements.

Each principle focuses on a specific aspect of tourism.

### *1. Travelling to natural destinations*

Eco-tourism involves purposeful travel to 'natural' destinations (as opposed to entirely human-made resorts), interacting with nature and gaining an understanding of natural history. These activities are carried out with as little alteration or disturbance to existing ecosystems as possible. 'Remote' areas (i.e. those that are furthest from large urban areas) are often used for eco-tourism. Such destinations are usually subject to environmental protection at international, national and/or local level (see Chapter 2). Nevertheless, an increase of eco-tourists to natural destinations can impact negatively on the environment (i.e. they exceed the limits of acceptable change).

**Activity Box 9: Eco-tourisms and eco-tourists**

The Responsible Travel website provides details of a number of holidays for eco-tourists. Refer to the definitions above and investigate the website in detail before undertaking the tasks below.

- Record brief details about four or five different types of holiday available on the website.
- Describe any differences in the types of eco-tourists these holidays are aimed at.
- In the first definition above, the focus is on eco-tourism, whereas the second focuses on the eco-tourist; which of these is most useful in relation to the holidays you have gathered information on (i.e. is the focus on the tourism or the tourist)?
- To what extent can each of the five holidays be considered sustainable? Explain your answer as fully as possible.

The increase in natural history programmes on terrestrial television and radio, and nature channels on satellite television (e.g. Discovery, National Geographic), has increased awareness of nature-based holidays.

*2. Minimising impact*

Eco-tourism endeavours to minimise its consumption of resources and to avoid some of the high-impact activities that have often taken place in mass tourism resorts (e.g. uncontrolled hotel construction). Eco-tourism aims to reduce environmental impacts through:

- the use of local building materials
- the construction of low-level architecture which matches the surrounding environment
- the use of renewable energy sources
- the reduction of water consumption
- the adoption of resource re-use and recycling strategies
- the monitoring and limitation or reduction of visitor numbers

(See, for example, Information Box 5.)

*3. Building environmental awareness*

Eco-tourism can involve experiencing and learning about nature. Educational strategies are therefore a key to building environmental awareness among tourists. These may involve the tour operator providing information about the local community for eco-tourists before departure and during their visit (see Information Box 5). Eco-tour guides may be trained in 'natural and cultural history, environmental interpretation and ethical principles' (Honey, 1999, p. 22). Codes of conduct for appropriate behaviour and dress may be provided for both tourists and tour operators. Information Box 5 summarises the attempts by Tribes Travel to minimise the impact of tourism.

*4. Providing direct financial benefits for conservation*

Tourism can provide opportunities to raise funds to benefit the environment, and can also make the conservation of natural resources beneficial to the local community. Funds can be raised through Park

**Information Box 5: Tribes Travel**

- Tribes Travel (established in 1998), in supporting the principles of environmentally sustainable tourism, is of the belief that tourism should be of socio-economic benefit to the local communities affected by it.
- Tribes Travel advocates respect for and working in co-operation with local communities and their environment. To attain this, local guides are employed, and locally owned and run services are used.
- Tribes Travel advocates keeping travel group sizes to a maximum of 12 in order to minimise impacts upon local communities and the environment and to reduce disturbance to wildlife.
- The company also takes its ethical stance further: all of the information for tourists about the local community and its culture is hand-made and printed in Nepal on environmentally-friendly paper.
- Tribes Travel has been designated the 'Most responsible tour operator' by Tourism Concern.

Source: Tribes Travel website.

**Activity Box 10: Learning about natural destinations**

Working individually, look at a series of natural history programmes featuring holiday destinations, and a variety of other sources (including Tribes Travel, Tourism Concern, Ecotourism Society, World Tourism Organization and World Travel and Tourism Council websites).

- For a specific region prepare a set of codes of conduct in relation to the natural environment and local people, addressing each of Honey's seven basic principles of eco-tourism.
- Think about sustainable ways of issuing the codes of conduct. For example, you could produce your codes of conduct as a pamphlet/leaflet to be sent out with tourist information brochures or as a web page.
- How else might you let travellers know that information is available – consider other methods of electronic communications available to you?

entrance fees, via voluntary contributions from tourists or in the form of tax revenue from tour operators, hotels, airlines and airports. These can then be directed towards conservation of species and habitats, as well as research and education (see 3 above). Other ways include organising holidays for which the visitor pays and carries out conservation work.

***5. Providing financial benefits and empowerment locally***

Multi-national tour operators can and do restrict local tourism income opportunities in favour of their own global businesses, resulting in a leakage of profits away from local communities and the loss of local community empowerment (see 7 below). To counter this the local community must be an empowered part of the planning, development, control and ownership of eco-tourism. In this way both the local community and the tourist have access to infrastructure such as reliable water supplies and sewage facilities. Members of the local community can be employed in tourism-related activities (e.g. providing accommodation, working as tour guides).

***6. Respecting local culture***

Eco-tourism aims to be less culturally intrusive and exploitative than mass tourism (see Case Study 3). It usually involves educating eco-tourists about local customs, practices, dress codes and appropriate behaviour (see 2 above). Eco-tourism that seeks simply to minimise impacts is described as 'light green', whereas 'deep green' eco-tourism involves positively promoting and revitalising local crafts, folklore, dance, music, theatre and museums – again with a minimum of intrusion. Case Study 3 summarises the Toledo Eco-tourism Association's attempts to adopt the principles of sustainability.

***7. Supporting human rights and democratic movements***

Another aspect of eco-tourism is opposition to undemocratic practices and violations of human rights. Often this means boycotting destinations where such practices take place. Sometimes it involves actively working to improve the political and economic conditions of communities. Tourism Concern has campaigned to stop inhumane treatment and improve the working conditions of local communities across the world; its campaign for the rights of porters in the Himalayas is summarised in Information Box 6.

Figure 9: TEA Villages and surrounding area.
Photos reproduced with permission of http://ecoclub.com/ toledo/.

## Case Study 3: The Toledo Eco-tourism Association

Belize offers tropical rainforest and coral reef as its resource base and has been a destination for tourists since 1965. The total number of tourist arrivals to Belize increased from approximately 30,000 in 1970 to 215,000 in 1990, and the government became concerned over the possible degradation of the natural environment. The government introduced a 5-year economic plan (1985-89) aimed at encouraging eco-tourism – a direct result was the work of the Toledo Eco-tourism Association.

Toledo is located in the southern-most region of Belize with the rainforest, the local culture and Mayan ruins as the tourism resource base (Figure 10). Here, one community-based organisation is committed to the principles of sustainable tourism.

In 1990 five villages in Toledo invested in establishing the Toledo Eco-tourism Association (TEA). Their aim was to plan and control eco-tourism in the area, regulate the number of tourists visiting each village and increase the region's economic base and standard of living. TEA projects have included the following:

- The development of restaurants, art and craft shops and museums, canoe, raft and motor boat trips and an eco-tourism trail in Garifun Village.
- The establishment of the Punta Gorda village trail project to help residents in a number of ways, including the protection of their land, the provision of employment and the generation of capital for a home site farmer's fund.
- The Laguna village guesthouse and meal plan, which has involved building tourist facilities using local materials, in the style of local traditional architecture. The Laguna project uniquely involves visitors consuming each meal with a different family, which spreads the economic benefits of tourism throughout the village.

In 1997, the TEA was still managed and controlled at grassroots level: 80% of the profits from tourism were directed to local service providers and 20% to the village aid fund (for the provision of services including health care, education, training programmes and conservation). As a result some village incomes had increased by 25%. Ten villages are now involved in the project

The TEA has faced a series of challenges: at the project's inception the government of Belize was reluctant to support it owing to the perception that Toledo lacked sufficient tourist infrastructure. Since the TEA was awarded the socially-responsible tourism prize in the late 1990s, national government interest has increased. The villagers did not, however, welcome this governmental interest because they perceived it as conflicting with the development of tourism ownership and management at a local scale.

Source: *Timothy and White, 1999; Southern Belize website.*

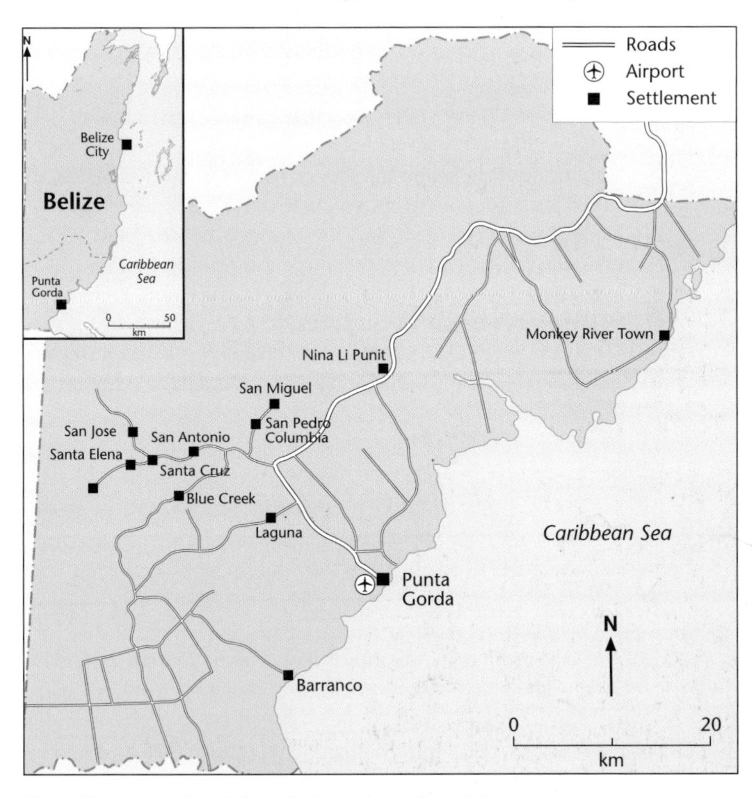


Figure 10: The location of the TEA villages in southern Belize.

### Activity Box 11: Applying Honey's principles of eco-tourism

Consider Honey's seven principles of eco-tourism in relation to the activities of Tribes Travel (Information Box 5) and the Toledo Eco-tourism Association (Case Study 3).

- Think about the benefits and the costs of each eco-tourism principle. How does each one *limit* the activities of such companies/organisations? How do they *enable* the company/organisation to extend its eco-tourism activities?
- Describe the ways in which each company/organisation could claim that it adheres to Honey's seven principles.
- In your opinion, why do these companies/organisations use their eco-tourist credentials to sell holidays and attract tourists?
- How might eco-tourism destinations, such as that in Toledo, Belize, become unsustainable over time? Refer to Butler's Model in Chapter 3.

### Information Box 6: Campaigning for porters' human rights

Figure 11: Nepalese porter walking dressed in a plastic bag instead of a rain jacket, 2001. Photo: © Jim Duff/IPPG.

There is evidence that the human rights of porters, who assist trekkers in the Himalayas, have been abused. Most Nepalese porters are poor farmers from lowland areas who, despite western perceptions, are not used to high altitudes and harsh conditions, and who cannot afford the correct climbing equipment or clothing.

Subsequently, for very low wages (approximately £2 per day), with no training, inadequate clothing and no insurance, porters have suffered frostbite, hypothermia, altitude sickness and even death. When they fall ill, porters have been abandoned by western tour groups; and during blizzards, when western tourists have been rescued by helicopter, Nepalese porters have been left behind.

Tourism Concern used 2002, the 'United Nations Year of Ecotourism' and the 'United Nations Year of Mountains', as the focus of their campaigns for porters' human rights. Guidelines, aimed at UK tour operators, on porters' rights and working conditions were devised jointly by Tourism Concern, tour operators and porters' protection groups. Tourism Concern has also issued 'Advice for Trekkers' to raise trekkers' and climbers' awareness of porters' human rights.

As a result of this campaign, tour operators are now providing essential protection, fair pay and working conditions to porters.

Source: *Tourism Concern website.*

### Activity Box 12: Tourism and human rights

- Investigate the Tourism Concern website and choose one example which indicates that tourism to a country has been affected in response to reports of human rights abuse.
- Set up a role-play in which different groups of up to four students represent the views of the government of the country, a tourism operator, a group of eco-tourists, the local community, an organisation such as Tourism Concern and any other interested parties. Each group should have a spokesperson, and one person should act as an independent adjudicator.
- Your aim is devise ways in which agreement can be made on overcoming the human rights abuses while establishing new opportunities for people to visit the country.
- Write a summary of your discussions as a news article for the Tourism Concern website.

### Eco-tourists

While Honey's seven principles help a tourist become an eco-tourist, no doubt you are thinking it would be useful to establish exactly what an eco-tourist is. Put simply, an eco-tourist is prepared to be educated about the place they are visiting and tends to be interested in the natural environment and in conservation issues. Increasingly, eco-tourists come from all groups of society (the younger, the working-class and the less wealthy as well as the older, the middle-class and the more wealthy), which means that eco-tourists cannot and should not be considered as homogenous. Mackay (cited in Holden, 2000) has produced profiles of eco-tourists with a big 'E' and a little 'e' (shown here in capitals and lower-case respectively for ease of reference). These tend to be related to an individual's commitment to environmental and sustainable principles, as Information Box 7 and Activity Box 13 demonstrate.

#### Information Box 7: The ECO-TOURIST and the eco-tourist

**'ECO-TOURIST'**

- ECO-TOURISTS are the smallest group to participate in eco-tourism.
- ECO-TOURISTS possess a deep ethical commitment to the environment – hence the term 'deep green'.
- This group includes the scientific researcher, or person who visits a destination for educational and/or conservation purposes.
- ECO-TOURISTS are likely to pay for holidays through specialist operators, such as Conservation International, Ecotour, or Eco-Escuela.
- An ECO-TOURIST is likely to stay in the same region for long periods, to endure harsher site conditions and to avoid consuming resources in a way that places a strain on the environment.
- Some ECO-TOURISTS, in fear of harming the environment, choose not to take holidays away from home.
- ECO-TOURISTS are often labelled 'deep green'.

**'eco-tourist'**

- The largest numbers of eco-tourist are those with a little 'e'.
- This 'light green' group is the most populous, and is positioned at the shallow end of the eco-tourism continuum.
- eco-tourists tend to have less interest in the principles of sustainability.
- This category includes people who travel to exotic destinations and accept simple and superficial overviews of their ecological impacts.
- This group expect a high degree of organisation within their tour and will probably book their tour through a high-street travel agent.
- The eco-tourist's environmental attitudes may extend to reading about sustainable issues and reducing water consumption.
- Comfort is chosen over and above conservation issues, and often the provision of western foods, accommodation and drink is expected.

### Activity Box 13: Profiling eco-tourists

Collect a range of tour operators' and other travel advertisements sourced from newspapers, magazines and the internet. Paste each advertisement in the centre of a sheet of paper and describe the type of tourist who might book through each operator. Compare your descriptions with the profiles in Information Box 7.

- Which of these are eco-tourists and which ECO-TOURISTS? Which are neither?
- Which holidays best describe an eco-tourist with a medium-sized 'e'? Write out a profile for one.
- Rank your advertisements and profiles from 'deep green' ECO-TOURISTS to tourists who do not appear to concern themselves with sustainable tourism at all. Describe the kind of tourism the latter group represents.
- In your opinion, is anything missing from the profiles? Is it useful to 'stereotype' eco-tourists in this way? How might you re-write or extend the profiles to take account of other tourism activities?

### Case Study 4: Costa Rican Eco-tourism

Figure: 12 Costa Rican rainforest. Photo: © Susana Cavallo

In the 1970s, Costa Rica was, by virtue of mainly attracting scientists, researchers, students and conservation groups, a deep-green eco-tourism destination. Its popularity increased in the 1980s, paradoxically because of extensive media exposure of the destruction of the tropical rainforests (Figure 12). Subsequent visitors, rather than having a deep interest in nature and the principles of sustainability, were mainly attracted to Costa Rica because it had become fashionable as a destination.

By the late 1980s the boom in tourism in Costa Rica had led to the expansion of adventure and activity holiday pursuits and the development of improved transport and higher-quality accommodation. Many Costa Rican tour operators moved into the profit-making 'eco-sell' category, but some of them sold nature-based holidays with little or no thought about the impact of larger volumes of visitors.

In the mid-1990s, partly because of poor central government planning and tourism policy, there was rapid and uncontrolled growth: more than 100 small hotels and restaurants, bars, casinos and night clubs were opened along the road leading to Manuel Antonio, Cost Rica's most famous National Park.

The move from deep green ECO-TOURISM to light green eco-tourism is still reflected in Costa Rican holidays featured in the brochures of many major tour operators. Light green nature excursions, including bird watching and visits to volcanoes, waterfalls, botanical gardens and National Parks (often via high-impact coach trips), have been over-promoted. Accommodation, rather than being low-impact, of an indigenous style and energy-efficient, belongs to multi-nationals, is ostentatious and includes western comforts and luxury (e.g. the Marriott Los Suenos).

Consequently, so-called eco-tourist destinations within Costa Rica appear in reality to be at the pioneering phase of mass tourism.

Sources: *Lumsdon and Swift, 1998; Honey, 1999.*

**Activity Box 14: Is eco-tourism sustainable?**

Case Study 4 indicates how tourism operators and others can eventually affect the viability of what was, initially, a deep green eco-tourist destination. First, look at the advertisements and the eco-tourist profiles you produced from Activity Box 13 and identify the types of tourists that would have visited Costa Rica in the 1970s, 1980s, 1990s and today. Second, think about this in relation to the approach of the Toledo Eco-Tourism Association (Case Study 3).

- Using Honey's seven basic principles of eco-tourism, consider what management strategies the Costa Rican authorities could adopt to ensure that future eco-tourism remains sustainable.
- Do you think deep green eco-tourism is sustainable in the long term? Give reasons for your answer.
- In your opinion is it necessary to ensure that eco-tourism in Costa Rica (for example) does survive? Give reasons for your answer.
- Do your answers to the above questions suggest possible tensions between eco-tourists and local communities? If so, in what ways?

The activities of eco-tourists are not always beneficial to their holiday destinations and the people that live there. As Holden's (2000) definitions indicate, both ECO-TOURISTS and eco-tourists are more likely to visit endangered environments, traverse new and delicate ecosystems (perhaps affecting endangered wildlife) and penetrate deeper into local communities. This contrasts strongly with mass tourism, which tends to concentrate within specially developed resorts and may have less impact on the environment and the local community. Nevertheless, eco-tourists often view their holidays as contributing towards sustainability. Honey has argued that, 'much of what is marketed as eco-tourism is simply conventional mass tourism wrapped in a thin veneer of green' (1999, p. 51). Tourism operators are not averse to using the notion of eco-tourism as a selling tool, when often the reality is very different.

**Eco-tourism or mass tourism?**

Though localities may be developed as destinations for eco-tourism with the best of intentions (e.g. be small in scale, slow growing, include the provision of environmental education and address such issues as conservation and the empowerment of local communities), the activities associated with eco-tourism can have devastating effects.

Where strict management and control is lacking, the problems associated with the initial stages of mass tourism may arise, including:

- exceeding carrying capacities through over-development (see Chapter 3, page 20-21, and Chapter 6), which can lead to environmental degradation
- changes to animal behaviour (e.g. the proximity of whale watching boats can result in distress to the whales)
- loss of resources and access to land (including the development of private beach resorts in, for example, Goa in southern India)

Furthermore, increased investment by multi-national corporations often results in leakages of tourism income away from the destination country (e.g. the take-over of Kenyan eco-lodges by the Hilton Group); it also compromises the ethics underpinning eco-tourism because the needs of large trans-national corporations are placed first. In extreme cases the exploitation of eco-tourism has involved cruelty to animals (e.g. the capture and display of jaguars by local farmers in Mexico) (Fennell, 1999). In many cases this involves a shift from deep to light green eco-tourism. Case Study 4 and Activity Box 14 help to illustrate the impacts of the exploitation of eco-tourism in Costa Rica.

The guiding principle behind eco-tourism is environmental and cultural sustainability in tourism planning, development and operation, and so is linked strongly with sustainable tourism (see Chapters 1 and 2). This assumes that mass tourism is unsustainable and eco-tourism is sustainable; whereas what this chapter has demonstrated is that both types of tourism are agents of development and change and both may exemplify sustainable and unsustainable practices. However, eco-tourism is here to stay – a fact reflected in the awarding of eco-labels and environmental awards, which is the focus of the next chapter.

# CHAPTER 5

# ECO-LABELS AND ENVIRONMENTAL AWARDS

As indicated in Chapter 2, the management of natural resources in tourist areas was traditionally based on a system of legislation. However, while regulations provide one way of protecting natural areas and improving environmental quality, in order to work they must be supported by other methods. Industry self-regulation through the use of eco-labels and green awards has a role to play. You may have noticed that some hotels and visitor attractions display eco-labels and environmental awards to indicate their increased commitment to sustainable approaches. As consumers have become more environmentally aware, the industry has reacted to varying degrees.

### Eco-labels everywhere

Everyone has seen eco-labels and environmental awards, even if we do not recognise them as such. Eco-labels tell us about the environmental claims of a product (think about labels on air fresheners) and can enhance the image of a company and increase the sales of a product. Labelling household products like CFC-free aerosols and dolphin-friendly tuna with their environmental credentials enables us as consumers to recognise, and choose to buy, those that do less harm to the environment.

Eco-labels have become popular in the tourist industry as a means of self-regulation. There are now a number of environmental awards and eco-labels, operating at local, national and international levels. In making a decision to stay at a hotel or visit a place because it has an eco-label or environmental award, we become eco-tourists. But, because different labels mean different things, eco-labels can sometimes confuse rather than help us make decisions. This chapter assesses a range of tourism-based eco-labels and environmental awards and encourages you to consider their use, purpose and recognition.

### The European Eco-label

A number of companies and organisations award eco-labels to tourism operators. Some awards, such as Green Globe 21 and the Tourism for Tomorrow awards (organised by the World Travel and Tourism Council), have become internationally recognised. But so many eco-labels now exist that their sheer number and variety can cause confusion. The European Eco-label for hotels, launched in 2003, is intended to alleviate this confusion. Its main aim is to help develop sustainable tourism by managing growth so as to avoid tourist accommodation causing environmental and social degradation.

The intention is that when tourists make a booking with a hotel displaying the European Eco-label logo (Information Box 8) they can be assured that it meets a number of environmental commitments set out by the European Commission. The hotel should provide:

> **'healthy lodgings, healthy nutrition and a healthy environment for the guests and the employees. Environmentally friendly tourist accommodation uses natural building materials, have non-smoking areas and avoid the use of hazardous chemicals. Linen is washed with more environmentally friendly detergents' (European Commission, 2003a).**

The European Eco-label is awarded only after an environmental audit led by a local representative – usually a government official (see Information Box 8). The first hotel in Europe to be awarded the European Eco-label was the Sunwing Resort at Kallithea in Rhodes, Greece, in September 2003 (Figure 13) (European Union, 2003). Activity Box 15 enables you to apply this tool to local businesses.

Figure 13: European Eco-label winner the Sunwing Resort, Kallithea. Photo: © Sunwing Resort Kallithea.

**Information Box 8: European Eco-label test**

The criteria shown here are used to audit how environmentally friendly a hotel's activities actually are. Once the hotel's eco-tourism level is established, it can consider applying for a European Eco-label.

***Evaluation***

The evaluator uses a numerical score to calculate whether the criteria have been met and to assess whether the business should receive a European Eco-label. Each item satisfied is worth one point. The scores are as follows:

| Resource/area of activity | Installation/provision of |
|---|---|
| Energy | Energy-efficient electrical equipment<br>Electricity from renewable sources<br>Appropriate thermal insulation<br>Automatic switch-off systems (light, heating, etc.)<br>Collection of energy consumption data |
| Water | Water-saving taps and showers<br>Water-saving dishwashers, washing machines, toilets etc.<br>Flexible change of towels and sheets<br>Appropriate waste water treatment |
| Staff training on | Environmental issues<br>Right dosage of detergents and cleaners<br>Effective waste, water, energy and resource management<br>Maintenance and servicing of the equipment |
| Information for guests on | Local environmental facts and news<br>Environmental measures taken at the accommodation<br>Ways to save water and energy<br>How to separate waste<br>Modes of public transport |
| Eco procurement (purchasing and supply) | Energy- and water-efficient equipment<br>Eco-labelled products<br>Refillable bottles<br>No disposable bottles, toiletries, cups, plates and cutlery |
| Dangerous chemical substances | Eco-labelled indoor paint, varnish and detergents<br>Appropriate use of chemical substances<br>Collection of chemical consumption data |
| Waste | Waste separation<br>Appropriate disposal of waste<br>Avoidance of disposable and hazardous products<br>Separation and disposal of hazardous waste |
| Others | No smoking areas<br>National Eco-label<br>Bioclimatic architecture<br>Food from local and organic farming<br>Use of photovoltaic (solar panel) energy and wind energy<br>Heat pumps, district heating, heat recovery<br>Use of rain and recycled water<br>Environmental management system or ISO 14001 (see page **) |

- Up to 9 points: No Eco-label awarded. More detailed information on the Eco-label is required before a full survey is allowed to go ahead.
- 10 to 20 points: The business is on the right track for the EU Eco-label. A full survey is required.
- 21 to 30 points: The EU Eco-label appears to be the right scheme to show guests how serious the business is regarding its environmental performance. Eco-label awarded.

Source: *European Commission, 2003b.*

**Eco-consumption**

Rural environments are important both for providing food and for attracting visitors. Tourism also influences, both directly and indirectly, the way that the countryside is managed. In July 2000 the UK Countryside Agency launched 'Eat the View' – a five-year initiative designed 'to raise public awareness and to secure more favourable market conditions to enable and encourage land managers to diversify and adopt more sustainable management practices' (Countryside Agency, 2004). This encourages guesthouses, hotels and restaurants to use local produce to help sustain local rural communities and the local identity.

Businesses gain because they work together: farmers can improve their marketing and work with suppliers to influence quality, quantity and choice. The use of local produce benefits the environment because shorter journeys result in less traffic congestion and air pollution. Less packaging is required, leading to a reduction in waste. The visitor benefits because fresher food requires less processing and often has a unique local taste. Information Box 9 describes how the use of local produce impacts on visitors, operators and farmers in Avon.

**Activity Box 15: Eco-labelling hotels**

Working in small groups, produce a set of questions that will allow you to carry out an environmental audit of a local business (where appropriate, refer back to your work on Center Parcs). Your questions can be based on the criteria shown in Information Box 8. You will have to decide a scoring system so that you can draw conclusions from the audit.

- Contact a local hotel or other accommodation provider and ask a senior representative of the business to answer your questions.
- Use the responses to assess how environmentally aware that particular business is.
- Compile a spreadsheet and ask each group to enter its data. Ask your tutor or the ICT provider to make the whole dataset available via a shared area, to allow every group to analyse the results. Consider:
  - whether any patterns emerge, and say why these might occur
  - whether there are any businesses that almost qualify for an Eco-label and how they could revise their practices to receive one
  - whether any businesses meet European Eco-label criteria, and, if so, whether they are aware of this (see above).

Where appropriate, contact businesses with the outcomes of your investigation. They may welcome the feedback, because adopting environmentally sustainable policies makes good business sense. By reducing its use of natural resources a business can benefit by reducing costs.

**Information Box 9: The Real Bath Breakfast**

Figure 14: The Real Bath Breakfast. Reproduced with permission.

The Real Bath Breakfast is an Agenda 21 initiative launched by the environmental charity Envolve (see References and Further Reading for websites). Its aim is to provide visitors to the city with a taste of local produce in hotel breakfasts. Hotels, guesthouses and restaurants displaying The Real Bath Breakfast logo (Figure 14) serve breakfast that has been prepared using produce from within 65km of Bath.

James (2002) has estimated that the average ingredients needed for an English cooked breakfast can travel up to 3298km (2050 miles) if they are purchased in a supermarket, whereas the ingredients for a 'Real Bath Breakfast', which are sourced locally, travel about 153km (95 miles) (Table 3).

**Table 3: Comparison of 'food miles' for The Real Bath Breakfast and the same foods purchased from a supermarket. Note: tea and coffee cannot be produced locally so Fair Trade products are used instead. Source: James, 2002.**

| Food Item | 'Food miles' travelled from source to table for: | |
|---|---|---|
| | The Real Bath Breakfast | Supermarket Breakfast |
| Bacon | 30 (48km) | 700 (1126km) |
| Sausages | 30 (48km) | 100 (161km) |
| Eggs | 6 (10km) | 100 (161km) |
| Tomatoes | 20 (32km) | 1000 (1609km) |
| Mushrooms | 6 (10km) | 50 (80km) |
| Bread | 3 (5km) | 100 (161km) |
| Total 'food miles' | 95 (153km) | 2050 (3298km) |

**Activity Box 16: Calculating the cost**

The Real Bath Breakfast example illustrates the importance of the relationship between tourism and the consumption of local food and drink.

- Approximately 900,000 visitors stay overnight in Bath each year. Using the figures shown in Table 3, calculate how many 'food miles' would be saved if each person consumed The Real Bath Breakfast rather than an equivalent one sourced from supermarkets.
- Food produced for The Real Bath Breakfast costs 5% more than breakfast ingredients sourced via a supermarket. Investigate the costs of a supermarket-sourced breakfast (based on a standard number of ingredients) and calculate how much more The Real Bath Breakfast costs in pounds and pence.

Investigate other examples of local or regional food initiatives in the UK, such as Taste of the West, and discuss the following questions:

- Why is local produce an important part of visitors' experience of a place?
- How successful do you think these schemes are in promoting local produce?
- Visitors' consumption of local produce obviously impacts on the environment. Could this be described as a form of eco-tourism?
- How could visitors' consumption of local produce be said to be a form of 'elitist' tourism?

## Environmental awards

The Tourism for Tomorrow awards were established in 1989 by the Federation of Tour Operators to help protect the environment.

The awards are now administered by the World Travel and Tourism Council and have been expanded to include industry partnerships and the training of employees. The two main ones for sustainable tourism are the Destination Award and the Conservation Award (see Tourism for Tomorrow website).

The 2002 entrants were asked to describe how their tourism project met one or more of the environmental and social objectives listed in Table 4.

**Table 4: The social and environmental objectives and evaluative questions of the Tourism for Tomorrow awards. Source: British Airways, 2002.**

| Objective | Questions |
|---|---|
| Social | How does your project improve quality of life for everyone in the community?<br>What contribution does your project make towards sustaining and preserving the social infrastructure, including health, education, poverty alleviation, culture and tradition?<br>How much influence does the local community have on the direction of your project and how are their rights protected? |
| Heritage | How does your project protect and enhance the built and natural heritage?<br>How has community infrastructure been improved and traditional building methods revived? |
| Management | How do you manage the project in terms of numbers of tourists and their impacts on waste, energy and water management? |
| Communication | How do you inform tourists and other stakeholders about the environmental and social implications of their activities before, during and after their visit? |
| Leadership | What is it that makes your project a role model?<br>What is innovative and environmentally unique about your project?<br>What lessons can other tourism operators learn from your project? |
| Sustainable tourism | How does your project contribute to a better quality of life for everyone now and for future generations? |

## Case Study 5: Skyrail – a multi-award winner

Skyrail is located in Queensland, Australia, between two of Australia's World Heritage Sites: the Wet Tropics World Heritage Area and the Great Barrier Reef. Skyrail offers panoramic views of the Australian tropical rainforest from 114 gondolas suspended 40m above the treetops on a cable that extends for 7.5km across the Barron Gorge National Park, making it the world's longest gondola cableway (Figure 15). It began operating in 1995 and can carry up to 700 passengers per hour in each direction.

Figure 15: Skyrail. Photo: Skyrail Rainforest Cableway.

These rainforests once formed part of a vast rainforest that covered the whole of the continent some 120 million years ago. The Barron Gorge National Park was designated a World Heritage Site in 1998. The Australian rainforests contain a rich diversity of plant and animal species, including 46 species of fern found nowhere else in the world, more than 40,000 insect species, 327 species of bird and 58 of frog. Rare species such as the Queensland tube-nosed bats, the leaf-tailed gecko and the Lumholtz tree-kangaroo live in the rainforests.

Skyrail is a good example of how significant tourist pressure can have minimal impact on the physical environment. Four viewing stations offer visitors the chance to use elevated boardwalks and viewing platforms. Because visitors travel above the canopy, their impact is kept to a minimum, and they also get a chance to see part of the rainforest that they would not normally see from the ground.

Skyrail was the first tourism company to be awarded both the Green Globe 21 and the Tourism for Tomorrow award. It also won the Queensland Tourism Awards for the best tourist attraction each year between 1996 and 1999, and is the most popular tourist attraction in northern Queensland.

Source: *Skyrail website.*

### Tour operators' initiatives

Tour operators may recognise the need for sustainable development but often lack the resources to maximise their sustainability potential. To overcome this, smaller companies can form coalitions. Examples include the Tour Operators Initiative and the Association of Independent Tour Operators (TOI and AITO – see their websites for further details). The principles they establish may include encouraging corporate commitment to sustainable development and management of tourism. TOI was developed *by* tour operators *for* tour operators and hopes that its principles will show consumers that the travel and tourism industry is actively working towards a sustainable future. Members of AITO are encouraged to gain the maximum number of stars for their sustainability activities. One star is given for signing up to AITO's responsible tourism policy; two stars for completing an environmental audit and putting a detailed policy in operation; and three stars for taking part in a specific responsible tourism project.

### Environmental quality awards

Environmental awards also take other forms. For example, environmental quality is an important issue in attracting people to beaches. One of the most recognised symbols of environmental quality at the seaside is the Blue Flag. The Blue Flag is a symbol of high environmental standards and of good sanitary and safety facilities at beaches and marinas (see the Blue Flag, Foundation for Environmental Education and Environmental Campaigns websites, page 52). The Blue Flag – the highest category for recognising beach quality – has been adopted in 24 countries across Europe and South Africa and has been awarded to nearly 3000 beaches and marinas (Figure 16). As with other awards, evaluation for a Blue Flag is based on specific criteria – 26 for beaches and 16 for marinas. Although the criteria are different for the two types of site, the same four aspects of management are covered:

1. Environmental education and information
2. Environmental management
3. Water quality
4. Safety and services.

Environmental Campaigns is also responsible for the UK Seaside Awards and the Keep Britain Tidy campaign (see websites – page 52). The UK Seaside Awards are concerned with water quality but also make a distinction between rural and resort beaches. They are only used in the UK.

#### Activity Box 17: Environmental awards – what's at stake?

First, focus on Case Study 5 and the Skyrail website.

- How fully does the information answer the questions on specific objectives shown in Table 4?
- Imagine you are to visit northern Queensland, would the awards given to Skyrail affect your decision to visit the rainforest? Give reasons for your response.
- Look at the descriptions of eco-tourists in Chapter 4 (page 30). Say which features of Skyrail an 'ECO-TOURIST' would take most account of in making a decision to visit the rainforest. Do the same for an 'eco-tourist'.

Next, consider why tourism companies, from small operators to multi-national corporations, might want to be involved in environmental awards. For example:

- How do tour operators, travel companies and tourism destinations benefit from receiving awards related to sustainable tourism?
- What might be the costs associated with their involvement?
- How far do you think environmental awards help improve tourists' confidence in the tourism industry's environmental practices? How far do you think they improve smaller tourism operators' confidence?

Finally, to what extent are environmental awards helpful in making decisions about visiting destinations or taking part in activities?

Figure 16: In the UK, beaches, such as this one at Woolacombe in Devon have received the Blue Flag awards.
Photo: Diane Wright.

**Activity Box 18: Presenting seaside awards**

Using the websites mentioned above as information sources, prepare a presentation that will:

- Describe the main differences between the Blue Flag and the UK Seaside Awards.
- Explain whether beaches that display one of these awards attract more visitors than those that do not, and the reasons for this.

Use a range of examples (from the UK and elsewhere) to illustrate your presentation. The presentation should be made in a format of your own choosing (e.g. a poster, a digital video, a *PowerPoint* slideshow or a cartoon storyboard), but must include the use of ICT and maps, images and illustrations.

Environmental groups have argued that the importance of some environmental awards and eco-labels may be limited because they act as marketing hype rather than reflecting real ecological and social values. The proliferation of eco-labels and awards can also cause confusion in people wishing to be eco-tourists. However, the tourism industry's interest in such awards demonstrates their usefulness in promoting environmentally sustainable tourism. What is needed is a clear system of eco-labelling that consumers can easily recognise and understand. You might like to think about the awards and eco-labels you have investigated and come to a consensus with your peers about what such a label would look like and what ethos would underpin it.

The next chapter looks at two tourism destinations: Malta and the Maldives. Both are island groups, both have experienced cycles of growth and decline in visitor numbers, and both have been the recipients of environmental and industry awards. The similarities end there – as you will discover.

# SUSTAINABLE TOURISM IN MALTA AND THE MALDIVES

This chapter examines the extent to which tourism operators, governments and local communities have adopted the principles of sustainability discussed in previous chapters. The focus of the first section is on cultural and heritage tourism in Malta as a response to mass tourism; the second section looks at the planned development of marine eco-tourism in the Maldives from the 1970s onwards.

Malta has historically offered cheap package holidays aimed at those seeking 'sun, sea and sand'; a drop in numbers visiting the islands in the 1980s led to the development of cultural and heritage tourism. The Maldives caters for tourists wishing to experience nature in a pristine and undeveloped environment. While both countries are small, their tourism activities illustrate different aspects of sustainable tourism and eco-tourism, but the application of planning models and practice display similarities.

## Alternative tourism in the Republic of Malta

### *Background*

The Maltese Islands of Malta, Gozo and Comino collectively known as the Republic of Malta lie in the Mediterranean Sea 368km north of Tripoli (Libya) and 93km south of Sicily (Figure 17). In 1998, the population of the Republic was approximately 375,000 (*Insight Guide to Malta*, 1999), living in an area of only 316km$^2$. Malta is therefore the most densely populated country in Europe.

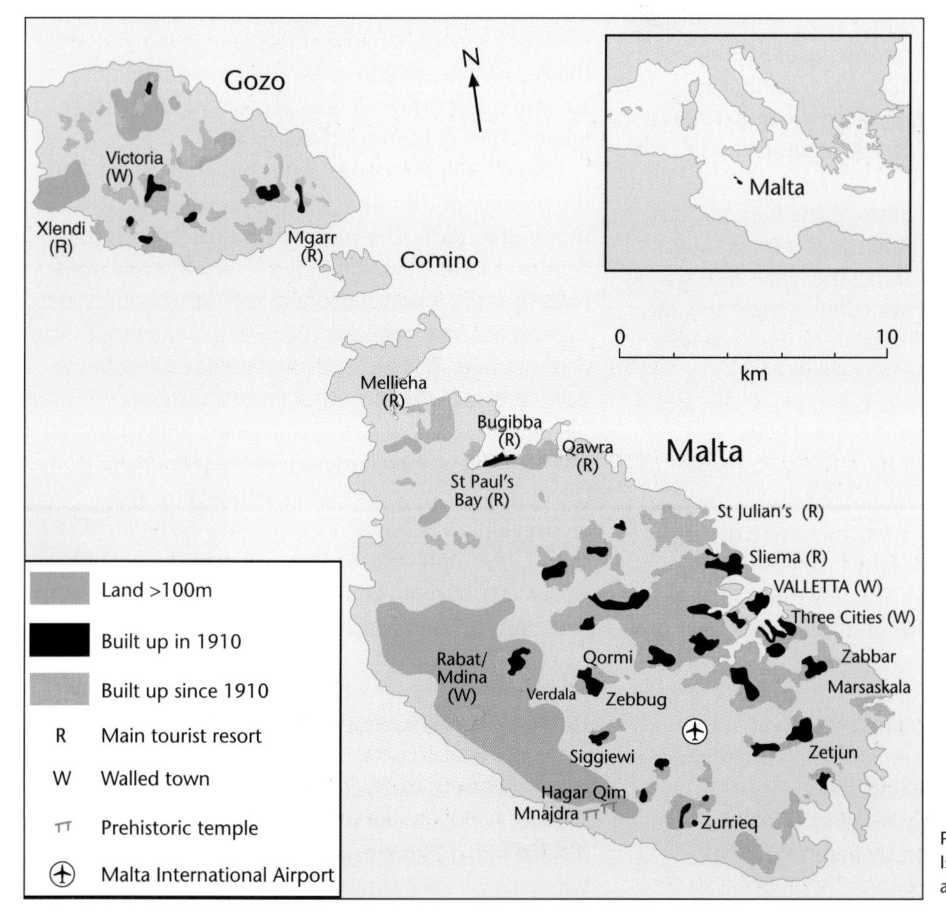


Figure 17: The Maltese Islands of Malta, Gozo and Comino.

The Republic of Malta has a unique culture which has been influenced by over 4000 years of colonialism. The Maltese associate their heritage with the Order of the Knights of St John, who ruled Malta from 1530 to 1798 and belonged to aristocratic families from all over Europe. The Knights were responsible for building Valletta (the capital) and left a rich legacy of baroque architecture. Most Maltese are devout Catholics, a fact reflected in the large number of Catholic churches scattered throughout the Republic and the widespread village religious processions or *festas* held between May and September each year.

The Islands came under British rule between 1800 and 1964, when they achieved independence. As a result, the culture shows a British influence, with British cuisine served widely and English used alongside Maltese as an official language.

International tourism is now the main economic activity of the Republic. In 1998, there were 1,182,240 international tourists, generating a gross income of ML254.4 million (£406 million) (National Tourism Organisation of Malta, 1999). (British military bases provided a source of income before 1964). Although the Republic of Malta has traditionally offered beach-based holidays, since the mid-1980s it has attempted to diversify towards cultural and heritage tourism.

Since the late 1950s tourism to the Republic has increased rapidly. As with other, similar mass tourism destinations (e.g. Greek Islands), the late 1960s was a period of uncontrolled construction of hotel and self-catering accommodation in Malta. At this time no planning mechanisms were in place to control speculative building, and only two trained planners lived there (Jones, 1971). During the 1970s government intervention in tourism development was more in evidence but tended not to involve the construction of associated infrastructure (e.g. adequate water supplies) for the increasing number of visitors (Oglethorpe, 1985). The downturn in arrivals that occurred between 1981 and 1984 could be attributed to several factors, including:

- the reduced aesthetic quality of the landscape caused by the unconstrained developments,
- environmental impacts, such as untreated sewage being released into bathing areas,
- the littering of coastal areas, and
- marine pollution caused by huge numbers of boat trips.

Concern over these issues, together with the dependency of its tourism industry on the British market and mass tourism, led the Maltese government to review its tourism policies in the early 1980s. In 1989 the government produced a Tourism Master Plan. This included a consideration of environmental and cultural impacts arising from tourism.

## Strategic planning in Malta

### *A brief history of tourism in Malta*

Malta's British connections mean that in the past its tourism industry has relied heavily on the UK market. This reliance was increased by the fact that Malta did not actively market its tourism product, but depended on a small number of UK tour operators to attract visitors. Mass tourism reached Malta in the mid-1960s owing to the introduction of package holidays, developments in aircraft technology and the Maltese government's own Development Plan objectives. Some tourist accommodation was created by renovating buildings formerly used as living quarters by British services personnel. Between 1965 and 1990 the Republic received visitors from more than 20 countries, but British visitors accounted for between 50 and 70% of tourist arrivals.

Since 1990 this dependency has abated – by 2000 the number of UK tourists to the Republic had dropped to 35%. The Maltese government's 1989 Tourism Master Plan also indicates a shift away from mass tourism, towards economically sustainable tourism, income generation and employment for local communities. This includes: market diversification to cultural breaks (holidays that involve watching religious festivals, military ceremonies, crafts and listening to traditional music); heritage tourism (holidays that involve viewing architecture and archaeological sites); and special-interest holidays (e.g. diving, golf, and visits to sites where Hollywood films were shot). The government also intended to attract fewer tourists, with each tourist spending more (e.g. by constructing higher quality more sustainable resorts) as well as targeting other nationalities (e.g. Eastern Europeans) (Markwick, 1999).

Malta worked with the World Tourism Organization towards strategic planning (WTO, 1994a). For the initial strategic analysis Malta was divided into 12 zones (ten on the island of Malta and two in Gozo – see Figure 17), roughly reflecting the

Figure 18: Images of heritage and cultural tourism in Malta. Photos: © Malta Tourism Authority.

Republic's areas of mass tourism. The analysis included:

- An **environmental analysis** to detect environmentally sensitive areas (e.g. agricultural, ecological and geological areas, insect and bird habitats) and place them under protection. This also included locating underground water aquifers to supplement the limited potable (drinkable) water supply.
- Investigating **tourist attractions** (e.g. towers, forts, palaces, traditional villages, major panoramic views and beaches) in terms of their carrying capacity. This was to determine whether overcrowding was occurring and, if so, whether it was having an impact upon the tourists' experience of the attraction.
- Mapping and surveying **existing areas of intensive tourism development** to determine whether further development would impact upon them. An evaluation of the quality of existing tourism development was also conducted.
- **Surveying and evaluating transport provision** helped to determine the quality, efficiency and organisation of the air and sea links, buses and taxis.
- Carrying out an **inventory of tourist accommodation** to determine the extent and quality of accommodation, and a projection of the extent and type of future accommodation requirements.
- An evaluation of **economic, environmental, and socio-cultural impacts** of further tourism.

This analysis enabled Malta to move into the second phase. Visions, goals and objectives were set, and strategies for achieving them included:

- Preventing the further spread of tourism buildings, with consideration given to development in existing built up-areas.
- Discouraging the construction of hotels of less than 4* standard (Markwick, 2001).
- Market diversification to attract a wider range of nationalities and higher-spending tourists. This was to be achieved by niche marketing of heritage and cultural tourism, sporting holidays (e.g. golf, diving), and conference tourism.
- Reducing seasonal tourism by attracting visitors to events throughout the year.

In its strategic planning, Malta also recognised the complex relationship between tourism and culture and heritage (Information Box 10).

Together the issues in Information Box 10 raise questions as to whether alternative forms of tourism are sustainable, particularly because they can give rise to tensions between the customs, behaviour, values and attitudes of locals and visitors.

The medieval and former capital of Malta, Mdina provides an ideal focus for looking at the cultural effects of 'alternative tourism'. Alternative tourism, in

### Information Box 10: The impacts of cultural and heritage tourism

Malta's Tourism Development Plan of 1989 included diversification to heritage tourism (involving archaeology, architecture), cultural tourism (involving cultural events, *festas*), sporting holidays and conference tourism throughout the year. This was based on the belief that these alternative tourist activities (some of which are eco-tourisms) could contribute to cultural sustainability, and there is evidence that they do.

- Inguanez (1988) explains how the presence of tourists has **enabled the revitalisation, rediscovery and escalation of tradition** (including parish *festas*, military ceremonies, folk events, filigree and lace making) and has led to an increased indigenous awareness of Malta's historical and architectural heritage.
- The performance for tourists of, for example, religious *festas* and military re-enactments – the **'commodification of culture'** – tends to cause the erosion of authenticity of the local culture, simply because symbols of national identity (e.g. costume, dance) become more exaggerated and elaborate in order to satisfy tourists. For the performers the symbolic meanings of cultural identity and customs may be reduced or lost altogether.
- A positive aspect of this **'staged authenticity'** is that performances take place in tourist 'front-regions' – so that communities in 'back regions' are spared the penetration of tourism. 'Front regions' are areas where local communities meet the tourist and where tourists are encouraged (e.g. museums, hotels), while the local community lives in 'back regions' (i.e. in private homes), which are out of bounds to tourists (MacCannell, 1976).
- Nevertheless, cultural and heritage tourism has implications for the local community in that it encourages tourists to **penetrate into private** spaces (e.g. inland rural areas), where people may be less accustomed to the presence of tourists.
- For the tourist this commodification of culture may result in what is termed **'emergent authenticity'**. Over time tourists tend to perceive these customs and cultures as authentic, even though often they are not.

### Activity Box 19: Towards eco-tourism in Malta

Using the information provided on Malta and material discussed in earlier chapters, carry out the following tasks:

- Use the tourism triangle (page 11) to describe cultural tourism in the Republic of Malta. Alter the shape to take account of all of the factors involved in cultural tourism: as well as taking account of the effects of tourists, local communities and the environment, add in the influence of international and government policies and the tourist industry.
- Look back at Butler's model (page 19) and think about how the Republic has progressed through the five stages of development. What stage is the Republic of Malta at today? Give reasons for your answer.
- Describe how useful the concept of zoning Malta has been for evaluating the impacts of tourism and developing a sustainable cultural tourism policy. How might the establishment of core and periphery zones in Malta be applied?
- Describe the negative and positive impacts of diversifying the Republic's tourism product towards heritage and cultural tourism and special-interest tourism (use Case Study 6: Mdina, and Information Box 10). Do you think that these tourisms, together with the Republic's marketing plans, will make Malta as a tourism 'product' sustainable?

## Case Study 6: Mdina: 'hidden Malta'

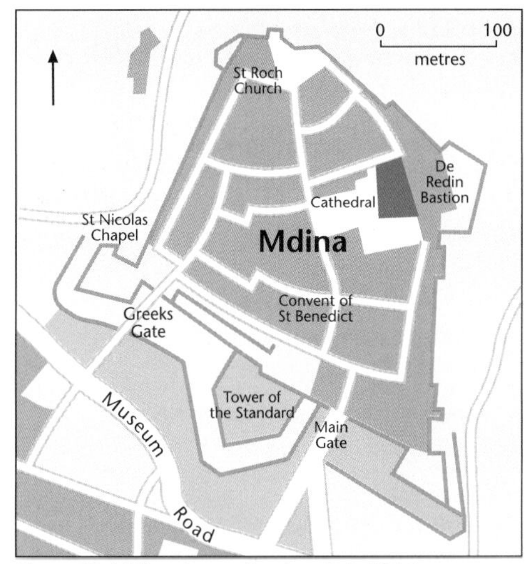

Figure 19: Mdina, the medieval capital of Malta.

Figure 20: A typical street in Malta's 'silent city', Mdina.
Photo: Chris Franklin, 2004.

Built during the medieval era, Mdina has an indigenous population of 200, and receives over 200,000 tourist visits every year (Markwick, 2001). In searching for an authentic 'hidden' Mdina, tourists have overwhelmed this small walled town.

In response to growing numbers of visitors, the local community has provided tourist attractions and services, which have resulted in the transformation of Mdina's interior space and the commodification of the town's heritage.

In 1998 there were already 30 commercial establishments catering exclusively for tourists. These included: souvenir shops, restaurants, tearooms, and themed multimedia exhibitions such as 'Medieval Times' and 'Mdina Experience'. While these 'infotainments' act as counter-attractions to the main tourist sites and encourage dispersal of tourists, they have also led to the growing intrusion of tourists into residential spaces. This has proved to be particularly problematic in the west and north-west of Mdina where the design of the traditional buildings is based on a central courtyard which is the focus of domestic life.

Residents have reported dismay as tourists peer through windows or even enter private homes. There have also been frequent complaints that visitors have used the winding, narrow alleys of the town to urinate, that tourists are sometimes indecently dressed, are noisy and/or leave litter.

The situation is worse during *festas* when large crowds of Maltese and tourists are drawn to Mdina. Similarly, flower festivals involve special displays, concerts, folklore events and re-enactments of historical events. The popularity of these occasions has resulted in tensions between tourists, the organising committees and local residents; with residents pointing out that they are rarely consulted about the problems caused by such events.

Charging tourists to enter the walled city has been suggested as one solution. Although this would offset some of the costs and pressures of tourism, it would not solve the problem of cultural tourism 'objectifying' the residents of Mdina and rendering them 'exhibits', in their 'museum' town.

After: *Markwick, 2001.*

**Activity Box 20: Investigating tourism first-hand**

For a named area in a city or town or small village that receives a number of visitors, you are to produce a report investigating the impacts of tourism. In your report you will need to identify:

- the most popular sites visited and suggest reasons for their popularity
- the types of visitor that are attracted to the location
- the types, number and distribution of commercial premises serving the requirements of visitors
- the attitude of the local community to the effects of tourism, both positive and negative
- examples of management by the local council and other groups to minimise the effect of tourism on the local environment and to promote sustainability
- possible ways in which the tourist location could be made more sustainable.

You should include results from questionnaires and interviews, maps, graphs, images and other illustrative material. Draw together your evidence and decide whether you think tourism in your chosen location is sustainable. It would also be useful to add quotes and references from the material in this book to support your case.

this case cultural tourism, encourages visitors to discover the 'hidden Malta' beyond the mass tourist resorts (Case Study 6). The result is an intrusive impact on the 'everyday' spaces of Maltese communities, especially within villages and small walled towns (Markwick, 2001), which you can investigate through Activity Box 20.

**Eco-tourism in the Maldives**

The Maldives Archipelago in the Indian Ocean consists of more than 1200 coral islands or islets, of which 420 are inhabited and 87 are resort islands. With the highest point of the islands being no more than 2.5m above sea level, the Maldives is the lowest country in the world. This means that the Maldives will be the first country to disappear as a result of any major rise in sea level.

The majority of visitors to the Maldives travel there by air. Air travel burns large amounts of fossil fuel and contributes to the amount of carbon dioxide in the atmosphere, which in turn contributes to global warming and rises in sea level. This means that the very act of visiting the Maldives puts the country's existence under threat. However, travellers can now calculate the amount of carbon pollution produced as a result of flying and offset their 'own' carbon emissions by helping to create forests, as Activity Box 21 demonstrates.

**Background**

The Maldives (Figure 21) has a sunny and tropical climate. Its scenic island beauty includes reefs, caves and canyons, and there are numerous attractive marine life. Tourism is the country's main industry, accounting for 20% of its GDP (followed by fisheries, trade and agriculture). The population of the Maldives Islands is approximately 270,000, and demonstrates African, Arabic and South-East Asian influences. Most Maldivians speak English (the country was a British Protectorate from 1887 to 1976), but the official language is Dhivehi (Indro-Indian).

The government-controlled and managed Maldives tourism industry has been carefully planned since its inception. Sustainable strategies include ensuring that the natural appearance of the islands is retained, and limiting tourism activity to a small number of quality resorts with a view to reducing cultural and environmental impacts. Tourism in the Maldives began in 1972 when there were only two resorts and 1000 visitors per year. By 1999 this had increased to 75 resorts with 200,000 visitors per year (Lonely Planet, 1997). The Maldives Ministry of Tourism website describes its vision for the Islands as:

> **'to be the best example of sustainable tourism development – a nation with an economically profitable tourism industry in harmony with its natural environment, cultural resources, and the values of its people.'**

**Marine tourism in the Maldives**

Marine tourism has increased in popularity at a faster rate than the tourism sector as a whole (Orams, 1999). It involves a range of activities including

**Activity Box 21: Becoming carbon-neutral**

Imagine you are travelling to the Maldives, but wish to become 'carbon-neutral' (see McKie, 2004) by compensating for the greenhouse gases your travel generates.

- Discover how far (and by what route) you would need to fly to reach the Maldives.
- Use the Future Forests carbon calculator (see websites) to work out how much carbon dioxide would be produced as a result of one return flight to the Maldives.
- The calculator offers you ways of compensating for your flights to and from the Maldives – i.e. ways of becoming carbon-neutral. Which would you choose and why?

adventure sports (e.g. diving), fishing and boating, and is usually defined as taking place in saline or tidal waters. The increase in popularity of diving in particular can be attributed to the development of diving equipment, the influence of the media, the increased demand for nature-based holidays and the reduction in the price of such holidays (Orams, 1999). In the Maldives, diving is available at numerous resorts including Meerufenfushi (Meeru) and Bandos (Figure 21).

Diving and other marine tourism activities offered in the Maldives by tour operators include: individual and group scuba diving in offshore areas to investigate wildlife, shipwrecks, and coral; diving cruises; scuba-diving courses; and near-shore marine tourism in the form of group and individual snorkelling, fishing, sea swimming, wading, boating (non-powered, motor and speedboats), glass-bottomed boat charters, island hopping, cruises, water taxis, canoeing, diving, wind-surfing, catamaran sailing, and beach volleyball (Figure 22).

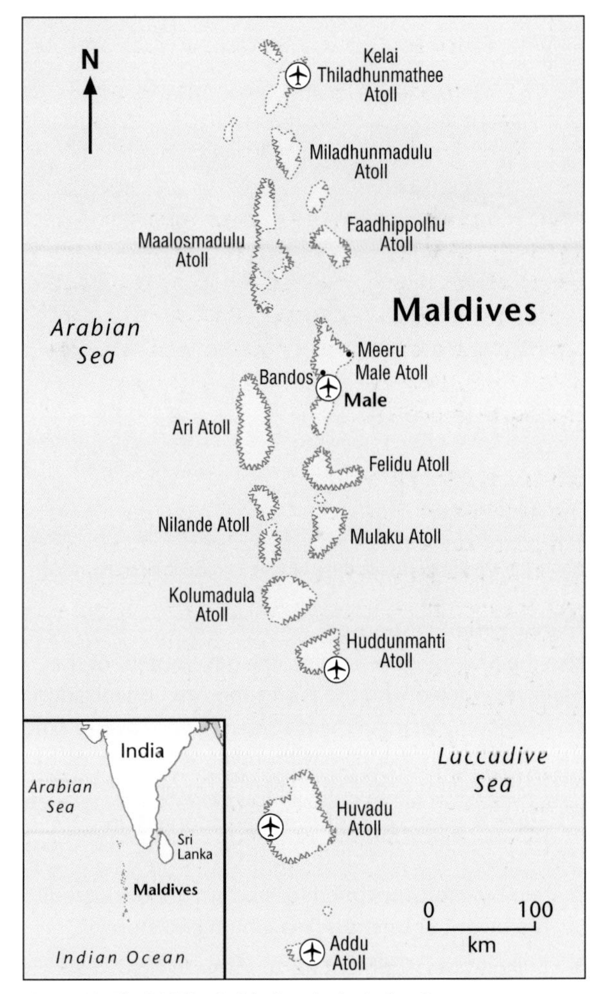

Figure 21: The Maldive Archipelago in the Indian Ocean.

*Tourism impacts*

Although there have been restrictions on tourism developments, the presence of large numbers of marine tourists, the use of marine technology and of finite resources have affected the marine environment.

Diving activities tend not to be environmentally friendly: coral breakages (especially of fragile branching species) are caused by contact with diving equipment. Inexperienced divers also tend to trample on and/or touch the coral. Such problems occur when tourists are not briefed or educated on the vulnerability of the marine ecosystem, and are exacerbated by the unregulated demand for scuba access to coral reefs by diving companies, keen to remain in business. Other damage has arisen from the removal of coral for hotel construction; the touching and feeding of fauna by tourists, and over-fishing by local communities, all of which conflict with the principles of sustainability. The negative primary and secondary effects resulting from marine tourism are summarised in Information Box 11.

Figure 22: Marine tourism in the Maldives. Photos: © Jason Poynting.

**Management responses**

Like the Maltese government, the government of the Maldives worked with the World Tourism Organization on developing management strategies intended to halt the decline in its marine environment. A number of different environmental management strategies (Chapter 3, page 20-23) have been adopted. In relation to resort development, these include:

- 'No buildings designed for tourism are to exceed the height of treetops (maximum two storeys)
- Building development for tourism cannot exceed 20% of each island's area
- All guestrooms must face the beach, but there must be at least 5m of beach from the front of the building to the shoreline' (WTO, 1994b, p. 164).

The Maldives tourism industry is also enforcing the following environmental and cultural standards:

- Using **local and natural materials** (e.g. wood) in the building of chalets, water bungalows and piers, to ensure they blend in with the local environment.
- Providing a reliable supply of water for consumption by **promoting the use of de-salinated rainwater, in order to conserve scarce groundwater.**
- Developing **sewage disposal systems** that do not eject untreated waste into the sea.
- **Educating the local community and tourists** about the disposal of litter. Tourists are encouraged to take their litter back to their hotels and apartments for recycling and to limit the amount of litter they produce.
- **Educating tourists at the resort and prior to departure about marine ecology**. They are told not to purchase turtle products, remove shale, sands and coral under any circumstances.

(Adapted from WTO, 1994b; Browning, 1999.)

**Information Box 11: Primary effects of marine tourism and consequent conditions (secondary effects). Source: Mason and Moore, 1998; Willliams, 1998; Crace, 1999; Hall and Page, 2002.**

| Primary effect of Marine tourism | Secondary effect of Marine tourism |
|---|---|
| Decrease in abundance and diversity of flora and fauna. | Change in the structure/composition of flora. Reduction or extinction of species of flora and fauna. |
| Change in fauna behaviour. | Fauna becomes stressed resulting in changed feeding and breeding habits. Fauna may occupy less desirable habitats. |
| Decrease in the aesthetics of the area. | Impairment of natural scene. |
| Decrease in water quality (e.g. from oil pollution from boats, hotel construction and run-off from resort areas). | Contaminated marine environment causing destruction of the natural habitat, coral and feeding grounds for fish. Possible death of flora and fauna. Impaired vegetation growth and susceptability to future damage. |
| Decrease in air quality. | Less attractive tourism environment. |
| Decrease in abundance and diversity of coral. | Impairment of natural scene. Less desirable location for marine tourism. Change in composition and structure of material. Increases risk of shore erosion. Endangers species dependent upon coral. |
| Decrease in quantity of surface and ground water supplies (diversion for local use to resort use — irrigation). | Decline in water availability for local domestic and agricultural use. |
| Increased sea and inter-island traffic (e.g. Maldives Island hopping) | Accidental importation of exotic species which may be damaging to local flora and fauna. |
| Overcrowding of sites/excessive visitation (increase in the number of divers/marine tourists). | Marine tourism environment less desirable. Aesthetics decrease. Impacts to flora and fauna. |
| Disturbance of near-shore aquatic life (most popular area of tourist interaction). | Change in structure/composition of flora and coral. Fauna becomes stressed. |
| Overloading of tourism developments for divers, and exceeding carrying capacity. | Impairment of natural scene. Aesthetics of area decrease. |
| Algal growth and eutrophication (from sewage). | Death of coral, impairment of natural scene/change in structure and composition of coral. |

The success of such strategies can be seen in the many awards the Islands have received. These include Green Globe 21 certificates and the Tourism for Tomorrow awards as well as other awards given by the Maldives Ministry of Tourism, tour operators and travel magazines (Maldives Ministry of Tourism website; and Chapter 5).

This section has demonstrated how sustainable planning for tourism is very important to the Maldives Government and how protection of the marine environment takes precedence over other considerations. It can be said that the Maldives is a good model of sustainable and eco-friendly tourism development.

**Activity Box 22: Managing marine tourism in the Maldives**

Both the Maldives Ministry of Tourism and the Maldives Promotion Board websites include information on the economic, environmental and cultural importance of marine tourism to the Islands. Using these and other sources mentioned in this book, devise your own investigation. Here are some suggestions:

- Produce a development plan outlining your recommendations to the Tourism Minister for promoting a resort based on sustainable principles. Think about the alternatives appropriate for such an environment and plan to attract one group. (If you choose to attract the deepest green ECO-TOURISTS; how might you ask them to compensate for their flight? How might they contribute to conservation projects on the Island? If you choose to go for attracting larger numbers of lighter green eco-tourists, describe what kinds of activities you must offer and how will you manage numbers.) Describe how you would minimise your resort's environmental impacts in line with the Maldives government's tourism plans described above.
- Investigate the benefits and costs of developing tourism for the local community. For example, use the Tourism Concern website to investigate how tourism is affecting Islanders' human rights, and devise a campaign to counter the adverse affects of tourism.
- Promoting sustainable marine tourism through campaigns and advice. For example, leaflets for visitors which detail sustainable tourism awards that the Maldives has won and describes the implications for protected areas; information for diving operators and their users – especially aimed at addressing the effects on flora and fauna summarised in Information Box 11.
- Think about the wider implications of tourism to the Maldives. For example, you might consider advising governments of other countries to encourage placing a levy on flights to the Islands and funding research into global climate change and sea-level rise, and/or considering more environmentally-friendly ways of travelling to the Islands. Who might you get to front your campaign?

You will be required to outline the results of your investigation to other members of your group, and hold a short plenary in the form of a question and answer session.

This chapter has shown how the development of alternative tourisms in the Maldives and the Republic of Malta have very different origins, but similar impacts upon the environment, local communities and their cultures. In the Maldives the increasing popularity of marine tourism (as a form of eco-tourism) affects the natural resource that the eco-tourist values most. The Maltese Islands have developed alternative responses to mass tourism, which include cultural and heritage tourism. This has resulted in conflicts between individuals, groups and organisations and has changed the way that Malta as a tourism 'product' is perceived. However, the governments and tourism authorities in both countries have worked with the World Tourism Organization to respond to increases in the numbers of tourists by attempting to attract relatively small numbers of wealthier, high-spending tourists. You might like to consider whether this, in itself, is a sustainable approach to tourism.

CHAPTER 7

# CONCLUSION

This book has identified how important sustainable tourism is to the future of tourist destinations and their immediate environments. Sustainable tourism is vital in managing the vast numbers of people who travel for pleasure and in minimising negative impacts. This not only benefits tourist-receiving areas but also the planet as a whole.

The future of sustainable tourism is difficult to predict. The use of eco-labels will continue to expand enabling consumers to become increasingly aware and demanding of environmental and ethical standards. That tourists are more aware of environmental and cultural problems caused by human action is manifest in the growing range of green consumerism, ethical investments and fair trade products. Therefore, the issue of managing tourists' interaction with the physical and cultural environments is a topical issue, but the question is how can it be resolved?

Generally, there is a lack of research in tourism ethics compared to the growing literature devoted to eco-tourism. In many cases the question of whether tourism is the most appropriate form of economic development also remains. The decision to develop an area for tourism should not be taken lightly, and alternatives that provide a balanced approach to economic development need to be considered. That is not to say that sustainable tourism is anti-tourism. If tourism is to develop it must be economically successful whilst protecting the very resources on which it depends.

Not all tourism can be regarded as unsustainable. As this book has shown the development of mass tourism can protect more sensitive areas which would be devastated by large numbers of visitors. But one of the major challenges is the pursuit of sustainable tourism in mass tourist-receiving areas. What is certain is a need to manage and influence the continued growth of tourism with a sustainable future in mind.

# REFERENCES AND FURTHER READING


British Airways (2002) *British Airways Tourism for Tomorrow Awards 2002 Brochure.* Waterside: BA.

British Tourist Authority (2001) *The Sustainable Growth of Tourism in Britain.* London: BTA.

Browning, G. (1999) 'The Maldives: a thousand miles from nowhere', *The Guardian - Travel supplement*, 27 November, pp. 2-3.

Butler, R. (1980) 'The concept of a tourism area cycle of evolutions: implications for the management of resources', *Canadian Geographer*, 24, pp. 5-12.

Center Parcs (2003) 'Center Parcs and the environment', *Student Information Pack.* Newark: Center Parcs Ltd.

Collins, B. (2000) 'Implementing environmental management systems in forest tourism; the case of Center Parcs' in Font, X. and Tribe, J. (eds) *Forest Tourism and Recreation: Case studies in environmental management.* Wallingford: CABI Publishing.

Cooper, C., Fletcher, J., Fyall, A., Gilbert, D. and Wanhill, S. (eds) (2005) *Tourism Principles and Practice* (third edition). Harlow: Longman.

Council for National Parks (1994) *Discover Your National Parks.* London: CNP.

Countryside Agency (2004) *'What is Eat the View?'* (www.countryside.gov.uk/LivingLandscapes/eat_the_view/What/index.asp) accessed 12 March.

Crace, J. (1999) 'Tourism', *Guardian - Education supplement*, 4 May, pp. 10-11.

Department for Culture, Media and Sport (1999) 'Tomorrow's Tourism' (www.culture.gov.uk/tourism/default.htm) accessed 12 July.

Ecotourism Society (1991) The Ecotourism Society Newsletter, 1,1.

English Tourism Council (2002) *'Background: Definition of Sustainable Tourism'* (www.wisegrowth.org.uk/default.asp?ID=S344L1P344I527) accessed 27 September.

European Commission (2003a) 'Environmental benefits of the European Eco-label' (www.eco-label-tourism.com/content/en_benefits.htm) accessed 23 November.

European Commission (2003b) 'Showing environmental responsibility' (www.eco-label-tourism.com/content/en_tour_operators.htm) accessed 23 November.

European Union (2003) 'Eco-Label News' (http://europa.eu.int/comm/environment/ecolabel/) accessed 23 November.

Fennell, D.A. (1999) *Ecotourism: An introduction.* London: Routledge.

Gratton, C. (1997) *Center Parcs: Ten years in the British tourist industry.* Sheffield: Leisure Industries Research Centre, Sheffield Hallam University.

Hall, C.M. and Page, S.J. (2002) *The Geography of Tourism and Recreation: Environment, place and space.* London: Routledge.

Holden, A. (2000) *Environment and Tourism.* London: Routledge.

Honey, M. (1999) *Ecotourism and Sustainable Development: Who owns paradise?* Washington DC: Island Press.

Inguanez, J. (1988) 'Tourism in Malta: a sociological view' in *Tourism for Malta - what future?* Proceedings of a Seminar Organised by the Centre for Social Research (Social Action Movement). 23 April.

*Insight Guide to Malta* (1999) Basingstoke: APA Publications.

James, K. (2002) 'Envolve: Partnerships for sustainability', lecture given at Bath Spa University College, 19 March.

Jones, H. (1971) 'A new deal for planning in Malta?', *Town and Country Planning*, 39, pp. 402-5.

Lonely Planet (1997) *The Maldives.* London: Lonely Planet (see also www.lonelyplanet.com).

Lumsdon, L.M. and Swift, J.S. (1998) 'Ecotourism at a crossroads: the case of Costa Rica', *Journal of Sustainable Tourism*, 6, 2, pp. 155-72.

MacCannell, D. (1976) *The Tourist: A new theory of the leisure class.* London: MacMillan.

McKie, R. (2004) 'Stardom is a gas for Brad and Leo', *The Observer*, 23 May (www.guardian.co.uk/climatechange/story/0%2C12374%2C1222903%2C00.html), accessed 12 July.

Mann, M. (2000) *The Community Tourism Guide.* London: Earthscan.

Markwick, M. (1999) 'Malta's tourism industry since 1985: Diversification, cultural tourism and sustainability', *Scottish Geographical Journal*, 115, 3, pp. 227-47.

Markwick, M. (2001) 'Alternative tourism: change, commodification and contestation of Malta's landscapes', *Geography*, 86, 3, pp. 250-3.

Mason, S.A. and Moore, S.A. (1998) 'Using the Sorenson Network to assess the potential effects of ecotourism on two Australian marine environments', *Journal of Sustainable Tourism*, 6, 2, pp. 143-54.

National Tourism Organisation of Malta (1999) *Tourism Statistics 1998*. Valletta: NTOM.

Newsome, D., Moore, S.A. and Dowling, R.K. (2002) *Natural Area Tourism: Ecology, impacts and management*. Clevedon: Channel View Publications.

Northumberland National Park Authority (2004) 'Sustainable Tourism Project' (www.northumberland-national-park.org.uk/AboutUs/VisitorServices/SustainableTourism.htm) accessed 12 July.

Oglethorpe, M.K. (1985) 'Tourism in a small island economy: the case of Malta', *Tourism Management*, 6, pp. 23-31.

Oliver, M. and Jeffrey, S. (2002) 'Earth Summit', *The Guardian*, 4 September (available online at www.guardian.co.uk).

Orams, M. (1999) *Marine Tourism: Development, impacts and management*. London: Routledge.

Owen, R.E., Witt, S.F. and Gammon, S. (1993) 'Sustainable tourism development in Wales: from theory to practice', *Tourism Management*, 14, 6, pp. 463-74.

Potter, R.B. and Phillips, J. (2004) 'The rejuvenation of tourism in Barbados 1993-2003: reflections on the Butler model', *Geography*, 89, 3, pp. 240-7.

Timothy, D.J. and White, K. (1999) 'Community-based ecotourism development on the periphery of Belize', *Current Issues in Tourism*, 2, 2-3, pp. 226-42.

United Nations Educational, Scientific and Cultural Organisation (2004) 'World Heritage Convention' (http://whc.unesco.org/pg.cfm?cid=160) accessed 12 July.

Williams, S. (1998) *Tourism Geography*. London: Routledge.

World Commission on Environment and Development (1987) *Our Common Future*. Oxford: Oxford Paperbacks.

World Tourism Organization (1994a) 'Tourism planning approach of Malta' in *National and Regional Tourism Planning: Methodologies and Case Studies*. London: International Thomson Business Press.

World Tourism Organization (1994b) 'Environmental management of tourism in the Maldives' in *National and Regional Tourism Planning: Methodologies and Case Studies*. London: International Thomson Business Press.

World Tourism Organization (2004) *WTO World Tourism Barometer*. Madrid, Spain: WTO.

Yarwood, R. (2002) *Changing Geography: Countryside conflicts*. Sheffield: Geographical Association.

## Useful Websites

Association of Independent Tour Operators – www.aito.co.uk
Blue Flag – www.blueflag.org
Conservation International – www.conservation.org
Countryside Agency – www.countryside.gov.uk
Department for Culture, Media and Sport (UK) – www.culture.gov.uk/tourism/tourism_policy/sustainable_dev.htm
Eco-Escuela – www.ecomaya.com
Ecotour – www.ecotour.org
Ecotravel.com – www.ecotravel.com
Environmental Campaigns – www.encams.org
Envolve – www.envolve.co.uk
European Commission (Eco-label) – www.eco-label-tourism.com
Future Forests – www.futureforests.com
Foundation for Environmental Education – www.fee-international.org
Green Globe – www.greenglobe.org
International Ecotourism Society – www.ecotourism.org
Maldives Tourism Promotion Board – www.visitmaldives.com.mv
Maldives Ministry of Tourism – www.maldivestourism.gov.mv
Malta Tourism Authority – www.visitmalta.com
National Geographic – www.nationalgeographic.com/travel/sustainable
Northumberland National Park Authority – www.northumberland-national-park.org.uk
Responsible Travel – www.responsibletravel.com
Seaside Awards – www.seasideawards.org.uk
Skyrail – www.skyrail.com.au/home.htm
Statistics on Tourism and Research UK – www.staruk.org.uk
Taste of the West – www.tasteofthewest.co.uk
Toledo Ecotourism Association – www.southernbelize.com/tea and http://ecoclub.com/toledo/lodge.html
Tourism Concern – www.tourismconcern.org.uk
Tourism for Tomorrow – www.tourismfortomorrow.com
Tour Operators Initiative – www.toinitiative.org
Tribes Travel – www.tribes.co.uk
United Nations Educational, Scientific and Cultural Organization – www.unesco.org
United Nations Environment Programme – www.uneptie.org/pc/tourism/sust-tourism/home.htm
World Heritage Sites (UNESCO) – http://whc.unesco.org
World Tourism Organization – www.world-tourism.org
World Travel and Tourism Council – www.wttc.org

## Curriculum Matrix

| Scales, places and environments | Example |
|---|---|
| Local coverage | Activity Boxes 19 and 21 (relating to students' local areas) |
| Regional/National coverage | Activity Box 3 (British ice sheet), Case Study 9 (North Staffordshire) |
| International coverage | Activity Box 2 (global distributions), Case Study 1 (Greenland), Case Study 4 (Alaska), Case Study 3 (Antarctica), Chapter 2 (global system) |
| Hazardous/polluted environments | Case Study 10 (moraine dammed lakes and mudflows), Activity Box 19 (hazards in the news), Chapter 6 (hazards) |
| Techniques in geography | Information Boxes 13 (ice-sheet modelling) and 14 (satellite remote sensing and GIS) |
| Environmental issues | Activity Box 6 (global warming and sea-level change), Case Study 2 (industrial pollution in ice cores), Chapter 2 (global system) |
| Skills in geographical enquiry | Activity Box 9 (laboratory experiment), Activity Box 14 (documentary research), Activity Box 15 (internet-based research), Activity Box 5 (map work) |
| Fieldwork | Activity Box 21 (local field work) |
| Environmental investigations | Activity Box 5 (sea-level change) |